PCAT® FLASHCARDS
Pharmacy College Admission Test

Premium Edition with Online Practice

Della Ata Khoury, CPhT

Research & Education Association
www.rea.com

Research & Education Association
61 Ethel Road West
Piscataway, New Jersey 08854
Email: info@rea.com

PCAT® Flashcard Book
Premium Edition with Online Practice, 4th Edition

Copyright © 2018 by Research & Education Association, Inc.
Prior editions copyright © 2013, 2010 by Research & Education
Association, Inc. All rights reserved. No part of this book may
be reproduced in any form without permission of the publisher.

Printed in the United States of America

ISBN-13: 978-0-7386-1237-9
ISBN-10: 0-7386-1237-5

LIMIT OF LIABILITY/DISCLAIMER OF WARRANTY: Publication of this work is
for the purpose of test preparation and related use and subjects as set forth herein.
While every effort has been made to achieve a work of high quality, neither Research &
Education Association, Inc., nor the authors and other contributors of this work guarantee the accuracy or completeness of or assume any liability in connection with the information and opinions contained herein and in REA's software and/or online materials.
REA and the authors and other contributors shall in no event be liable for any personal
injury, property or other damages of any nature whatsoever, whether special, indirect,
consequential or compensatory, directly or indirectly resulting from the publication, use
or reliance upon this work.

PCAT® is a trademark of Pearson Education, Inc., or its affiliates. All other trademarks
cited in this publication are the property of their respective owners.

Cover image © iStockphoto.com/andresr

REA® is a registered trademark of
Research & Education Association, Inc.

Table of Contents

About Our Author

Della Ata Khoury, CPhT, B.S., B.A., M.A., is a pharmacy technician instructor and externship coordinator at LARE Institute in the greater Boston area. She holds the distinction of being among the first nationally certified pharmacy technicians in Massachusetts. In 2015, she was one of just 14 experts chosen by the Pharmacy Technician Certification Board to develop new test content for the Pharmacy Technician Certification Exam.

Della worked as a hospital pharmacy technician for 12 years, through 2010, before turning her focus to pharmacy technician training and certification.

She holds a master's degree in regional economics and social development, a B.A. in political science, and a B.S. in biological sciences, all from the University of Massachusetts–Lowell.

Della is an active member of the Pharmacy Technician Educators Council and the Massachusetts Society of Health-System Pharmacists.

About REA

Founded in 1959, Research & Education Association (REA) is dedicated to publishing the finest and most effective educational materials—including study guides and test preps—for students of all ages.

Today, REA's wide-ranging catalog is a leading resource for students, teachers, and other professionals. Visit *www.rea.com* to see a complete listing of all our titles.

Acknowledgments

We would like to thank Pam Weston, Publisher, for setting the quality standards for production integrity and managing the publication to completion; Larry B. Kling, Vice President, Editorial, for his overall direction; Alice Leonard, Production Editor, for project management; John Paul Cording, Vice President, Technology, for coordinating the design and development of the online REA Study Center; Ellen Gong for proofreading; and Jennifer Calhoun and Transcend Creative Services for typesetting revisions.

Welcome to the World of Pharmacy

Applying to pharmacy school is the first step toward a rewarding career. Our *PCAT Flashcards (4th Edition)* is an excellent way to ensure you'll do well on the Pharmacy College Admission Test and are able to pursue any of a number of professional paths, ranging from community pharmacy to drug research, from government service to medical and scientific publishing.

About the PCAT

The PCAT was developed to help screen pharmacy school applicants by assessing the general and scientific knowledge needed for pharmaceutical education. The better your score, the better your chances of getting into the school of your choice.

This computerized exam contains five timed subtests: Writing, Biological Processes, Chemical Processes, Critical Reading, and Quantitative Reasoning.

Overview of the PCAT

PCAT Subtests	Number and Approx. Percentage of Item Types
1. Writing (30 minutes)	**1 prompt**
2. Biological Processes (40 minutes)	**48 items**
General Biology	50%
Microbiology	20%
Human Anatomy and Physiology	30%
3. Chemical Processes (40 minutes)	**48 items**
General Chemistry	50%
Organic Chemistry	30%
Basic Biochemistry Processes	20%
Rest Break: 15 minutes (not included in total test time)	
4. Critical Reading (50 minutes)	**48 items**
Comprehension	30%
Analysis	40%
Evaluation	30%

(continued)

PCAT Subtests	Number and Approx. Percentage of Item Types
5. Quantitative Reasoning	**48 items**
Basic Math	25%
Algebra	25%
Probability & Statistics	18%
Precalculus	18%
Calculus	14%
Total Test (205 minutes): 192 multiple-choice items, 1 writing prompt	
n.b.: Each multiple-choice subtest contains 40 operational (scorable) items and 8 experimental (non-scorable) items.	

Today's PCAT, based on the 2016-2017 test blueprint, has undergone critical shifts in test coverage. The Biological Processes and Chemical Processes subtests have added passage-driven items that present specific problems, research issues, or novel situations that for instance may focus on a research study or experiment. Other noteworthy changes include added coverage of genetics, health, and physiology on the Biological Processes section, while Chemical Processes questions now address basic biochemistry processes but de-emphasize questions requiring identification of nomenclature. The Critical Reading subtest continues to contain science-related passages but now also has passages on humanities and the social sciences. The Quantitative Reasoning subtest has added coverage of ratios and contains more items that present a word-problem or problem-solving scenario. For more information on the PCAT and to schedule your test, visit Pearson's official test site at *http://pcatweb.info*.

About This Book

REA's *PCAT Flashcards (4th Edition)* is the ideal supplementary resource to help you ace the Pharmacy College Admission Test. Its flashcard-style practice sets have been completely updated to reflect the latest PCAT test blueprint.

Developed by a leading educator in the field, the book is designed to help you raise your score in the final days before the test. It gives you hundreds of PCAT-like multiple-choice questions with clear, context-rich explanations to help you rapidly close your knowledge gaps.

The book comes with four online quizzes with instant diagnostic reports to brush up your remaining weak spots. Taking our online quizzes also gives you a better feel for test-day conditions for this computer-based test. Look for the STOP sign at the end of each practice section in the book as your cue to take your next quiz at the REA Study Center (*www.rea.com/studycenter*).

With your admission to the pharmacy college of your choice on the line, the 205-minute PCAT can feel daunting. Let our handy on-the-go prep help you approach the exam with confidence.

Good luck on the PCAT!

Permissions

Permission has been sought and granted for the use of the following passages:

Lindsey Helm, PharmD: *Types of Insulin – What Is the Difference?* https: www.pharmacytimes.org/landing/855

Anthony M. Boyd, John S. Clark, and Stan S. Kent: *Strategic Thinking in Pharmacy*; American Journal of Health-System Pharmacy, July 2017, 74 (14) 1103–1108: DOI: https://doi.org/10.2146/ajhp160356; Originally published in *Strategic Thinking in Pharmacy* in 2017, American Society of Health-System Pharmacists, Inc. All rights reserved. Reprinted with permission.

Jeannette Y. Wick, RPh, MBA, FASCP: *Drug Shortage: Unexpected Reward,*; Republished with permission of Intellisphere, LLC, From Jeannette Y. Wick, RPh, MBA, FASCP; Jan. 1, 1969; permission conveyed through Copyright Clearance Center, Inc.

Adam Martin, PharmD.: *Be the Change You Wish to See in Pharmacy,* Republished with permission of Intellisphere, LLC, August 14, 2017; permission conveyed through Copyright Clearance Center, Inc.

Jacob Stratman, Ph.D.: *Zora Neale Hurston (1891–1960),* CLEP American Literature, 2nd Edition, REA, Inc., copyright © 2015, p. 115

Lynn Marlowe, M.A.: *Lyndon Johnson's Great Society,* CLEP History of the United States II, 1965 to the present, 2nd edition, REA, Inc., copyright © 2013, pp. 138–139

Dawn Hogue, M.A., *Becoming An Empathetic Reader, AP English Language and Composition Crash Course,* REA, Inc. 2017, pages 141–142

Lynn Marlowe, M.A., *The Plains Indians, CLEP History of the United States II, 1865 to the Present,* REA, Inc. 2016, page 141 (adapted text)

Laurie A. Callihan, Ph.D., *Homeostatic Mechanisms, Total Solution for the GED Test,* 2nd Edition, REA, Inc. 2017, page 421

Section I

Biological Processes

DIRECTIONS: Each of the questions or incomplete statements in this section is followed by four suggested answers or completions. Select the one that is best in each case.

Questions

Q–1

The main abiotic source of carbon in the environ-ment for the carbon cycle comes from

(A) carbon dioxide in the air.

(B) carbon dioxide in water.

(C) carbon monoxide in the air.

(D) carbon monoxide in water.

Your Answer _____

_____

Q–2

The optimum pH and body site for amylase activ-ity is

(A) 2, stomach.

(B) 5, small intestine.

(C) 7, oral cavity.

(D) 8, stomach.

Your Answer _____

_____

Answers

A–1

(A) In the carbon cycle, CO_2 circulates between the living and nonliving sectors of an ecosystem. CO_2 composes 0.04 percent of the atmosphere. Producers (plants) in food chains fix it into the protoplasm of plants via photosynthesis. The element moves through the other trophic levels by nutrition and eating. Respiration by consumers and decomposers returns it to the abiotic sector, air, from the biotic sector, living organisms.

A–2

(C) The interior of the stomach has a pH of 2, which is necessary for the action of pepsin. The surface of the skin has a pH of 5.0 to 5.5. The pH range of the small intestine's lumen includes pH=8. The pH of the oral cavity is usually about 7, which is necessary for the action of salivary amylase, which begins the digestion of starch.

Questions

Q–3

Hydrolysis of lipid molecules yields

(A) amino acids and water.

(B) amino acids and glucose.

(C) fatty acids and glycerol.

(D) glucose and glycerol.

Your Answer _____

_____

Q–4

Unlike prokaryotic cells, eukaryotic cells have

(A) a cell membrane.

(B) cytoplasm.

(C) a DNA molecule.

(D) a nuclear membrane.

Your Answer _____

_____

Answers

A–3

(C)   Hydrolysis is a type of chemical digestion. When fatty acids are hydrolyzed, the process
yields fatty acids and glycerol. Amino acids are the
digested building blocks of proteins. Glucose is a
subunit of carbohydrates. Water molecules are required to split chemical bonds in hydrolysis but are
not produced in the process.

A–4

(D)   Eukaryotic cells have their genetic material encased in a defined membrane, the nucleus.
Prokaryotic cells (bacteria and blue-green algae)
are more primitive, less complex cells than eukaryotic cells of other species. They do, however, possess all the listed structures except (D).

Questions

Q-5

The least amount of useful energy flowing through a food chain is available to the

(A) herbivores.

(B) producers.

(C) secondary consumers.

(D) tertiary consumers.

Your Answer _____

_____

Q-6

Enzymes affect biochemical reactions by

(A) destroying all substances produced in the reactions.

(B) raising the temperature of the reaction's environment.

(C) reversing their direction.

(D) accelerating the reaction rates.

Your Answer _____

_____

Answers

A–5

(D) Producers intercept rays of light energy from the sun to conduct photosynthesis. With each succession through the link of a food chain, less energy becomes available for use to run the metabolic processes of the organisms in a particular trophic level. Thus there is less energy available to the herbivores than there is to the plants, the producers. Succeedingly less remains for the secondary and tertiary consumers.

A–6

(D) Enzymes are organic catalysts, speeding up chemical reactions of living systems by accelerating the attainment of reaction equilibria by lowering the activation energy of the reaction. Enzymes are specific to the reaction they catalyze and the substrates they bind to. They are not used up in the reaction itself.

Questions

Q-7

Simple squamous tissue is a type of which of the following kinds of tissue?

(A) Connective

(B) Epithelial

(C) Muscle

(D) Nerve

Your Answer _____

_____

Q-8

The ten-inch human-body tube accepting swallowed food is the

(A) esophagus.

(B) larynx.

(C) nasal cavity.

(D) pharynx.

Your Answer _____

_____

Answers

A-7

(B) Epithelial tissue covers the free surfaces of the body. For example, simple (one cell layer) squamous (flat, platelike) epithelial tissue can be found on the surface of the skin, and acts as a protective barrier. Muscle tissue consists of muscle fibers, and contains no simple squamous tissue. Nerve tissue is made almost entirely of neurons and neuroglial cells. Connective tissue, such as bone, blood, and tendons, contain cells that are separated by and suspended in some sort of matrix. Vascular tissue is not a valid tissue category.

A-8

(A) The other choices are respiratory tract structures.

Questions

Q–9

The majority of ATP molecules derived from nutrient metabolism are generated by (the)

(A)   anaerobic fermentation and glycolysis.

(B)   fermentation and electron transport chain.

(C)   glycolysis and substrate phosphorylation.

(D)   Krebs cycle and electron transport chain.

Your Answer _____

_____

Q–10

Mitosis functions in many organism life cycle events EXCEPT

(A)   body cell replacement.

(B)   development.

(C)   gametogenesis.

(D)   growth.

Your Answer _____

_____

Answers

A-9

(D)   Only a small fraction of ATP molecules is produced from anaerobic process of fermentation or glycolysis. Once pyruvic acid is formed, its entry into the aerobic Krebs cycle unleashes most of the original glucose molecule's energy. Krebs cycle reactions yield high energy electrons (oxidation) that are then shuttled down a series of transport acceptors located in the inner mitochondrial membrane until they finally combine with oxygen and H^+ to form water. During electron transport, a proton gradient is generated across the inner mitochondrial membrane. The collapse of this proton gradient provides energy for the production of ATP molecules from ADP molecules and inorganic phosphates.

A-10

(C)   Mitosis produces body cells whereas meiosis is the cell division process yielding gametes or sex cells: gametogenesis.

Questions

Q–11

RNA is made by the process of

(A) duplication.

(B) fermentation.

(C) replication.

(D) transcription.

Your Answer _____

_____

Q–12

Insulin is produced by the _____ and regulates the metabolism of _____.

(A) liver... proteins

(B) pancreas... proteins

(C) liver... carbohydrates

(D) pancreas... carbohydrates

Your Answer _____

_____

Answers

A–11

(D) This is a rote-memory question. Duplication or replication refers to DNA copying.

A–12

(D) Insulin is produced by the beta cells of the pancreas. This hormone regulates the metabolism of carbohydrates by removing excess glucose from the blood and stopping the use of fat as an energy source.

Questions

Q–13

Two parents are heterozygous and display respective blood types A and B. If they mate, the probability of producing an offspring with blood type O is

(A) 0%.

(B) 25%.

(C) 50%.

(D) 75%.

Your Answer _____

_____

Answers

(B) The blood type A parent is $I^A i$ and the blood type B parent is $I^B i$. Since they are both heterozygous, each must be a carrier of the recessive O type. Use of probability shows any one of the four blood types occurring among offspring with equal probability, thus 25% for O, A, B, or AB. Also, using a Punnett square, it is found that the 4 genotypes, $I^A I^B$ (AB), $I^A i$(A), $I^B i$ (B), ii (O) occur in equal ratio.

	I^A	i
I^B	$I^A I^B$	$I^B i$
i	$I^A i$	ii

Questions

Q-14

The human condition of color-blindness is

(A) caused by a recessive allele.

(B) equally common in both sexes.

(C) expressed by a heterozygous genotype in females.

(D) inherited by males from their fathers.

Your Answer _____

_____

Pharmacists can be controversial: Today, some pharmacists across the country are refusing to fill prescriptions for birth control and morning-after pills, saying that dispensing the medications violates their personal moral or religious beliefs. (www. washingtonpost.com)

Answers

(A)   Many of the better-known sex-linked human conditions, such as hemophilia and color-blindness, are caused by recessive alleles. Sex-linked (X-linked) genes are located on the X-chromosome. Thus males, whose sex chromosomes are X and Y, have only one such gene. Assuming that there are only two alleles for this X-linked gene, males are genotypically either C—(normal) or c—(i.e., color-blind). The Y-chromosome does not carry any encoded genes in this case. Therefore males need to inherit only one gene for colorblindness to be color-blind. For females, whose sex chromosomes are X and X, three genotypes are possible: CC, Cc and cc. A woman of genotype Cc is a carrier of the disease but does not express the recessive effect of color-blindness. She can, however, pass on her recessive allele to her offspring. In order to produce a color-blind female (cc), a female carrier would have to mate with a color-blind male (c—). Each parent offers a C allele on the X chromosome for a c genotype in the offspring. This is unlikely and an infrequent event.

An example of a common cross is:

$$Cc \times C—$$

	(female)	(male)
	C	c
C	CC	Cc
—	C—	c—

One-half of the males produced are color-blind. One-half of the females produced are a carrier.

Questions

Q–15

All are common forms of energy used in metabolism EXCEPT

(A) chemical.

(B) heat.

(C) kinetic.

(D) nuclear.

Your Answer _____

_____

Q–16

Genes control body chemistry by ultimately specifying the structure of

(A) carbohydrates.

(B) lipids.

(C) phospholipids.

(D) proteins.

Your Answer _____

_____

Answers

A–15

(D)   Chemical energy is stored in the bonds of biomolecules: sugars, lipids, etc. Heat is a by-product of any chemical conversion of metabolism. Light energy drives photosynthesis, and kinetic energy is the energy of motion. Animals move, generating this kinetic energy from conversion of chemical bond energy.

A–16

(D)   DNA serves as a template for RNA synthesis and RNA serves as a template for protein synthesis. Proteins participate in a wide variety of body chemistry. For instance, as enzymes they catalyze nearly all chemical reactions in biological systems. They serve as transport molecules such as oxygen-carrying molecules, hemoglobins and myoglobins. They protect our bodies against foreign pathogens in the form of antibodies.

Questions

Q–17

The gene that turns structural genes off and on in an operon is the

(A) cistron.

(B) operator.

(C) promotor.

(D) regulator.

Your Answer _____

_____

Q–18

The variable portion of a DNA nucleotide is at its

(A) base.

(B) deoxyribose.

(C) phosphate group.

(D) ribose.

Your Answer _____

_____

Answers

A–17

(B)   In an operon, the operator gene is adjacent to the first of several consecutive structural genes that code for enzymes that are needed for a particular metabolic pathway. These structural genes are often arranged in the same order that the enzymes which they code for are used in the pathway. The promotor is located next to the operator gene, opposite the side of the linked structural genes and is the location at which the RNA polymerase, which generated the RNA that is necessary for enzyme synthesis, binds. The regulator gene is at another location on the chromosome. This location can be near or far from the operon that it regulates.

A–18

(A)   The base: adenine (A), cytosine (C), guanine (G) or thymine (T) varies from nucleotide to nucleotide building block in a DNA strand. Any DNA nucleotide is occupied by only one of these bases for four possible nucleotide structures. The other choices are constant in the nucleotide. Ribose is a component of an RNA nucleotide.

Questions

Q–19

Select the cell type containing the highest concentration of mitochondria.

(A) Erythrocyte

(B) Leukocyte

(C) Muscle

(D) Neuron

Your Answer _____

_____

Q–20

The smallest, most specific category of classification is the

(A) family.

(B) genus.

(C) phylum.

(D) species.

Your Answer _____

_____

Answers

A–19

(C) Muscle cells are the engines of an animal, developing contractile pulling forces to produce work. Mitochondria, cell powerhouses that extract energy from nutrients, are most in demand here.

A–20

(D) The hierarchy of classification levels is, from most general down to most specific:

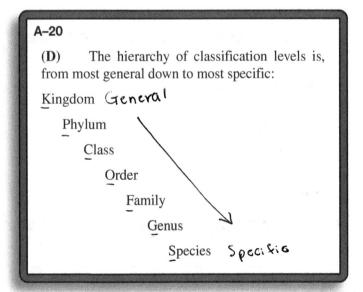

Kingdom General
 Phylum
  Class
   Order
    Family
     Genus
      Species Specific

Questions

Q-21

The largest, most general category of classification is the

(A) class.

(B) genus.

(C) kingdom.

(D) phylum.

Your Answer _____

_____

Q-22

As muscles become stronger, muscle cells change by

(A) expanding.

(B) contracting.

(C) multiplying.

(D) rigidifying.

Your Answer _____

_____

Answers

A–21

(C) Refer to the scheme in A-20.

A–22

(B) As muscles become stronger, muscle cells increase in volume.

Questions

Q–23

Which of the following nucleotide bases is found only in RNA?

(A) Thymine

(B) Uracil

(C) Guanine

(D) Adenine

Your Answer _____

_____

A qualified pharmacist can also teach in colleges of pharmacy, supervise the manufacture of pharmaceuticals, or get involved with the research and development of new medicines. With more academic work, pharmacists can move into pharmacology, become pharmaceutical chemists, or combine pharmaceutical and legal education to pursue jobs as patent lawyers or consultants on pharmaceutical and drug laws.

Answers

A–23

(B)   In RNA, uracil is present. Its counterpart in DNA is thymine, which is not found in RNA.

Questions

Q–24

A human birth defect produced by a sex-linked recessive allele of a gene is

(A) albinism.

(B) diabetes mellitus.

(C) hemophilia.

(D) high cholesterol.

Your Answer _____

_____

SSRIs, or selective serotonin reuptake inhibitors, are a widely used class of antidepressants that came under scrutiny during a drug-safety controversy several years ago. (Encyclopedia Britannica, 2005.)

Answers

(C)   Two well-known examples of recessive sex-linked traits in human beings are red-green color-blindness and hemophilia. These recessive sex-linked traits occur in a higher frequency in men than in women.

Albinism is an autosomal recessive disease. An individual heterozygous for albinism appears normal because one normal gene can be sufficient for making enough of the functional enzyme that makes melanin pigments. Albinism is associated with low melanin levels.

Diabetes mellitus is characterized by an elevated level of glucose in blood and urine and arises from a deficiency of insulin. The causes for the disease are not clear but there is evidence that this defect has a molecular basis as indicated by abnormally formed insulin.

High cholesterol level is a genetic disease resulting from a mutation at a single autosomal locus coded for the receptor for LDL (low-density lipoprotein). Whether a trait is dominant or recessive does not apply to this disease because the heterozygotes suffer from a milder problem than the homozygotes. The heterozygotes possess functional LDL receptors, though they are present at a deficient level.

Questions

Q-25

The skin performs all of the following human body functions EXCEPT

(A) protection.

(B) sensation.

(C) storage.

(D) temperature regulation.

Your Answer _____

Q-26

The biceps brachii produce movements by pulling on

(A) bones.

(B) joints.

(C) muscles.

(D) nerves.

Your Answer _____

Answers

A–25

(C) A study of skin structure reveals skin's ability to perform all but one of the listed capabilities, i.e., blood vessels to vent body heat, receptors to sense stimuli, and layers to protect the body.

A–26

(A) The biceps brachii are the muscles on the ventral portion of the upper arm that pull and bend the forearm. Bones are the rigid bars that yield to skeletal muscles' pulling force. Movable joints allow a source of mobility between articulating bones. Skeletal muscles are stimulated by nerves. Lacking this stimulation, they will not respond.

Questions

Q–27

Neurons that conduct signals away from the central nervous system are classified as

(A) afferent.

(B) associative.

(C) internuncial.

(D) motor.

Your Answer _____

_____

Q–28

The innermost layer of the eye is the

(A) choroid coat.

(B) cornea.

(C) retina.

(D) sclera.

Your Answer _____

_____

Answers

A-27

(D)   Sensory or afferent neurons send signals toward the central nervous system (CNS). Associative, or internuncial, neurons are within the CNS. Motor or efferent neurons, with axons outside and directed away from the CNS, send signals out to peripheral points.

A-28

(C)   The retina contains the receptor cells that receive and register incoming light rays. The choroid is a middle layer of darkly pigmented and highly vascularized tissue. This structure provides blood to the eye and absorbs light to prevent internal reflection that may blur the image. The outer sclera (white of the eye) includes the transparent cornea. The pupil is an opening in the donut-shaped, colored iris interior to the cornea.

Questions

Q–29

Which of the following is NOT a polymer?

(A) DNA

(B) Glycogen

(C) Glucose

(D) RNA

Your Answer _____

_____

Q–30

Which law explains the inhalation and exhalation of air in terms of pressure changes?

(A) Archimedes' law

(B) Dalton's law

(C) Boyle's law

(D) Mendel's law

Your Answer _____

_____

Answers

A–29

(C)   A polymer is a long complex molecule formed by the bonding of simpler, repetitive subunits. DNA and RNA are polymers of nucleotides. Glycogen is a polysaccharide. Polysaccharides are polymers of simple sugars, including glucose. Glucose is a subunit, not a polymer.

A–30

(C)   Boyle's law states that air pressure is inversely proportional to volume. As the chest cavity increases due to the flattening of the diaphragm and rib elevation, internal pressure drops below that of the atmosphere, causing an inrush of air.

Questions

Q–31

The highest pressure of circulating blood is found in a(n)

(A) arteriole.

(B) artery.

(C) capillary.

(D) vein.

Your Answer _____

_____

Q–32

Which of the following is part of a human's axial skeleton?

(A) Clavicle

(B) Fibula

(C) Humerus

(D) Rib

Your Answer _____

_____

Answers

A–31

(B) Blood flows through the circulatory system due to a pressure gradient. The blood will flow from a region of higher pressure to one of lower pressure. Therefore, blood pressure must be greatest at the beginning of the blood's circuit, namely, the aorta, which is an artery.

A–32

(D) The rib is one of the twelve pairs of bones that form a rib cage to protect the lungs and heart. Along with the skull and vertebral column, the rib cage forms the axial skeleton. The bones of the paired appendages as well as the pectoral and pelvic girdles belong to the appendicular skeleton.

Questions

Q-33

Glial cells

(A) conduct signals.

(B) contribute to movement.

(C) cover the skin.

(D) support neurons.

Your Answer _____

_____

Q-34

Select the disease caused by a protozoan.

(A) Chicken pox

(B) Common cold — viruses

(C) Malaria

(D) Measles

Your Answer _____

_____

Answers

A–33

(D) Glial cells bind neurons together. They offer nerve cells support, protection, and nutritional supply.

A–34

(C) Malaria is caused by protozoans of the genus Plasmodium, of the class Sporozoa. The other choices represent diseases caused by viruses.

Questions

Q–35

Which of the following has a vitamin as a building block?

(A) Apoenzyme

(B) Coenzyme

(C) Holoenzyme

(D) Protein

Your Answer _____

_____

Q–36

The filtering of inhaled debris that travels through the upper respiratory tract occurs through the action of

(A) cilia.

(B) goblet cells.

(C) Leidig cells.

(D) villi.

Your Answer _____

_____

Answers

A-35

(B) All enzymes are composed primarily of protein. The more complex enzymes have non-protein portions called cofactors; the protein portion of the enzyme is called an apoenzyme. If the cofactor is an easily separated organic molecule, it is called a coenzyme. Many coenzymes are related to vitamins. An enzyme deprived of its vitamin is thus incomplete, leading to the nonexecution of a key step in metabolism. Holoenzyme refers to the RNA polymerase, with its core enzyme and sigma subunit associated together.

A-36

(A) Cilia line the upper respiratory tract, waving against air inflow to filter out unneeded debris. Villi are finger-like extensions of the membranes of cells lining the small intestine. They increase surface area to facilitate absorption of digested nutrients. Goblet cells line the same region and secrete mucus. Leidig cells are in the male testis.

Questions

Q-37

Substances in the blood are transported across the nephron tubules by mechanisms in the process of

(A) filtration.

(B) osmosis.

(C) reabsorption.

(D) secretion.

Your Answer _____

_____

Q-38

A person receives the results of a hematocrit during a series of blood tests. A hematocrit is the

(A) abundance of white blood cells in blood.

(B) concentration of sugar in the blood.

(C) level of circulating antibodies.

(D) percentage of blood cellular material by volume.

Your Answer _____

_____

Answers

(D) Filtration first moves blood plasma substances from the glomerulus (capillary) into the cuplike Bowman's capsule at the nephron's origin. After monitoring these solute concentrations (e.g., glucose, sodium, etc.), reabsorption returns them to the blood from the nephron tubule at high percentage rates. Secretion is a third step, moving materials from the blood (peritubular capillaries) to the distal convoluted tubule for exit and elimination.

(D) Hematocrit is the percentage of blood cells in blood by volume. For males this value is normally 47±5; for females, it is 42±5. Thirty-two percent is abnormally low, indicating anemia — a diminished capacity of the blood to carry oxygen.

Q–39

The relatively large size of the mammalian brain, allowing for greater learning, association, and memory, is due to the enlargement of the

(A) cerebellum.

(B) hypothalamus.

(C) cerebrum.

(D) midbrain.

Your Answer _____

_____

The discovery that sulfa drugs could cure serious illnesses was a major step forward for medicine. These drugs, also called sulfonamides, are made in the laboratory, mostly from a crystalline compound called sulfanilamide. They are classified as antibiotics: drugs that stop the growth of or destroy infectious organisms in the body.

Answers

(C)   The brains of all vertebrates are divided into the hindbrain, midbrain, and forebrain. In lower vertebrates, such as fish, the hindbrain is the dominant portion of the brain. It consists of the medulla oblongata and pons. The former deals with vital reflexes, such as cardiac activity, and it links the spinal cord to the rest of the brain. The latter contains the respiratory center, and like the former, it is the origin of many cranial nerves. The cerebellum is also part of the hind brain: it functions in equilibrium and proprioception (awareness of body/limb position and movement).

The midbrains of fish process visual information and their forebrains function in olfactory (smell) sensation. These sensory functions are attributed to the cerebrum in higher vertebrates.

The midbrain is relatively small in humans, and, as the origin of several cranial nerves, it controls eye movements and pupillary size.

In all vertebrates, the forebrain consists of the diencephalon and the cerebrum. The diencephalon consists of the thalamus, a relay center for sensory input en route to the cerebrum, and the hypothalamus, which regulates many activities, including circadian rhythms, body temperature, emotions, food intake, and some hormone secretion. The cerebrum is highly developed in mammals: it constitutes 7/8 of the human brain. The cerebrum functions in learning, association, and memory. Birds also show great development of the cerebrum.

Questions

Q–40

In humans, there are many anatomical adaptations that function to increase surface area for chemical reactions and transport mechanisms. All of the following are examples EXCEPT

(A)   the alveoli of the lungs.

(B)   the microvilli of the small intestine.

(C)   the villi of the small intestine.

(D)   the sensory hairs (cilia) in the cochlea of the inner ear.

Your Answer _____

_____

Statins are drugs like Zocor and Lipitor that block (inhibit) an enzyme the body needs to produce cholesterol, thereby lowering blood cholesterol levels. (www.webmd.com)

Answers

(D) Alveoli are tiny thin-walled air sacs within the lungs. There are widespread sheets of capillaries that cover the alveoli. The millions of alveoli in each lung increase the surface area through which gases can diffuse between air and blood.

The small intestine has many adaptations that increase its surface area for both digestion and absorption (transport of nutrients from the lumen into the blood or lymph). First, the small intestine is very long (about 12 feet); second, the inner layer, or mucosa, is folded into villi that project into the lumen. Microvilli, which are folds of the epithelial cells composing the villi, further increase the surface area. Microvilli are also referred to as the brush border. There are brush border enzymes that complete chemical hydrolysis of nutrient molecules. Then the small monomers formed are absorbed.

Questions

Q–41

The period of human gestation is divided into three trimesters. The event that is correctly matched to its trimester of occurrence is which of the following?

(A) The third trimester is characterized by development and differentiation.

(B) The greatest growth in size occurs in the first trimester.

(C) The limb buds develop in the first trimester.

(D) Organ development begins in the second trimester.

Your Answer _____

_____

Q–42

Name the bone that does NOT articulate with the humerus.

(A) Clavicle

(B) Radius

(C) Scapula

(D) Ulna

Your Answer _____

_____

Answers

A-41

(C) Human embryonic development takes nine months; these months are divided into three trimesters of three months each.

In the first trimester, cleavage and implantation occur within the first week. The embryonic membranes begin to develop, followed by gastrulation (the differentiation of the three primary cell layers: ectoderm, mesoderm, and endoderm) and neurulation (formation of the neural tube). By the end of the first month, organ development has begun—these organs include the eyes, heart, limb buds, and most other organs. In the second month, morphogenesis occurs. Morphogenesis refers to the development of form or structure. In short, the first trimester is a critical period of differentiation and development, but growth is not pronounced.

The second trimester is a period of rapid growth in size and weight. The mother may become aware of kicking from the baby. Growth continues and is most prominent in the final trimester.

A-42

(A) The humerus, or the upper arm bone, articulates with the radius and ulna (forearm bones) at its distal end. Its other end fits into the lateral socket of the scapula, or shoulder blade. It does not articulate with the clavicle, or collarbone.

Questions

Q–43

Smoking cigarettes over a long period harms the upper respiratory tract's

(A) alveoli.

(B) cilia.

(C) goblet cells.

(D) villi.

Your Answer _____

_____

Q–44

Eye receptors and their function can best be summarized as

(A) cones–color discrimination, rods–twilight vision.

(B) cones–twilight vision, rods–color discrimination.

(C) ganglia–color discrimination, rods–twilight vision.

(D) lens–light refraction, cornea–light refraction.

Your Answer _____

_____

Answers

(B)   Cells that line the upper respiratory tract have cilia. These cilia trap and filter foreign debris. Alveoli, which would also be harmed by smoking, are in the lower respiratory tract. Villi and goblet cells are located in the small intestine.

(A)   Rods and cones are retinal cells lining the eye's inner surface. Cones are specialized for color discrimination or visual activity. Rods are utilized in dim light.

Questions

Q–45

Among humans, a universal recipient is a person that has which blood type?

(A) A+

(B) AB+

(C) AB–

(D) O+

Your Answer _____

Q–46

Humans, great apes, and monkeys are all members of which of the following taxonomic categories?

(A) Genus

(B) Family

(C) Order

(D) Species

K
P
C
O
F
G
S

Your Answer _____

Answers

A-45

(B) A person of blood type AB has no anti-A and no anti-B antibodies in his blood plasma. Therefore, there will be no antibodies present that would attack foreign red blood cells that enter the bloodstream during transfusion. A person whose blood has a positive Rh-factor also has no antibodies that attack Rh antigens present on red blood cells. Therefore, a person of blood type AB+ would have no trouble in receiving any type of blood during a transfusion.

A-46

(C) All are members of the order of Primates.

Questions

Q-47

Following menses, the initiation of the menstrual cycle follows an increase in the secretion of the hormone

(A) ACTH.

(B) FSH.

(C) LH.

(D) GnRH.

Your Answer _____

_____

Q-48

The two criteria used most of ten in taxonomic classifications are

(A) color and height.

(B) evolution and lifespan.

(C) lifespan and morphology.

(D) morphology and phylogeny.

Your Answer _____

_____

Answers

A–47

(B)   The concentration of follicle-stimulating hormone, or FSH, increases following menses. Thus, the menstrual cycle continues. It is secreted by the pituitary gland and serves to increase follicle growth around a selected sex cell in the ovary.

ACTH = adrenocorticotrophic hormone
LH   = luteinizing hormone
GnRH = gonadotrophin-releasing hormone

A–48

(D)   Morphology refers to body structure and form while phylogeny represents evolutionary history. The two are related. For example, a chimpanzee is the most humanlike animal because of the recent common evolutionary ancestor of chimp and human, revealed by the fossil record.

Questions

Q–49

Cells that sense sound are found in the ear's

(A) cochlea.

(B) pinna.

(C) semicircular canals.

(D) vestibule.

Your Answer _____

_____

Q–50

Blood normally circulates through vessels in which sequence?

(A) Artery – arteriole – capillary – venule – vein

(B) Arteriole – artery – capillary – vein – venule

(C) Capillary – arteriole – artery – vein – venule

(D) Vein – capillary – venule – artery – arteriole

Your Answer _____

_____

Answers

A–49

(A) This is a snail shell-shaped structure in the inner ear. The semi circular canals (dynamic equilibrium) and vestibule (statice equilibrium) are there to control body balance. The pinna, outer ear cartilage flap, transmit sound waves from the outer ear through the middle ear and on to the inner ear.

A–50

(A) Arteries take blood away from the heart, dividing into smaller, more numerous arterioles. They divide to become numerous, microscopic capillaries for exchange with cells. They collect into venules, which merge to form larger veins. Venules and veins return blood to the heart.

Questions

Q-51

Which of the following statements is true?

(A) In prophase, the sister chromatids separate.

(B) In telophase, the nuclear membrane begins to form.

(C) In metaphase, the sister chromatids begin condensation.

(D) In anaphase, the chromosomes move to the spindle equator.

Your Answer _____

_____

Cholesterol is an important fatlike substance (lipid) that is made in the liver and is necessary for the body to function. (www. webmd.com)

Answers

A-51

(B) Mitosis is the phase of the cell cycle during which one cell divides into two. Strictly speaking, mitosis refers to division of the nucleus. Cytokinesis, or cytoplasmic division, follows immediately. There are four consecutive stages of mitosis: prophase, metaphase, anaphase, and telophase.

In prophase, the chromosomes become visible as the sister chromatids condense into rod-like bodies. The nuclear membrane disintegrates and the nucleolus disappears. Microtubule spindles begin their formation.

In metaphase, the spindle attaches to the centromeres (central constricted region of each chromatid). Chromosomes are guided by spindle microtubules to the spindle equator, the central plane of the cell.

In anaphase, the sister chromatids of each pair separate and move from the equator to opposite poles of the cell. This movement is perpetuated by the depolymerization of the microtubule apparatus.

Telophase is simply a reversal of prophase: the nuclear membrane and nucleolus begin formation, and the chromosomes decondense into thread-like forms. Cytokinesis follows or occurs simultaneously and the bilobed cell with two nuclei will split into two individual cells.

P
M
A
T

Questions

Q–52

A subject with Type A blood

(A)   has A antibodies in his plasma.

(B)   has B antigens on his red blood cells.

(C)   can successfully receive blood from a type O person.

(D)   can successfully receive blood from a type AB person.

Your Answer _____

_____

Low-density lipoprotein (LDL) is called "bad cholesterol." (www.webmd.com)

Answers

(C) The ABO blood system is based on the presence of antigens on the red blood cells and antibodies in the plasma. A type A person has A antigens on his red blood cells and anti-B antibodies in his plasma. He cannot have anti-A antibodies in his plasma as they would cause his red blood cells to agglutinate (clump). A type B person has B antigens and anti-A antibodies. A type AB person has both A and B antigens, and therefore has no antibodies, while a type O person has no antigens and therefore has both anti-A and anti-B antibodies.

Concerning blood transfusions, a risk exists when a recipient's plasma antibodies agglutinate the donor's cell antigens. There is no risk associated with the recipient's cell antigens being agglutinated by the donor's plasma antibodies, because those antibodies are diluted by the recipient's plasma.

A type A subject can only receive blood from another type A person or from a type O person, since the anti-B antibodies in the type A's subject plasma will not have anything to agglutinate. If the type A person were to receive blood from a type AB subject, his anti-B antibodies would agglutinate the B antigens from the donor's blood.

Another important group of blood antigens is the Rh factor. Someone with the Rh factor is designated Rh+. Those without the Rh factor are designated Rh–. Unlike the ABO blood groups, no antibodies are normally present, unless the blood has been exposed to the Rh antigen. There can be no prediction of the Rh blood type for the type A subject in question, as the two groups are independent.

Questions

Q–53

Synapsis

(A)   occurs during the second meiotic division.

(B)   refers to the pairing between homologous chromosomes.

(C)   is synonymous with chiasmata.

(D)   refers to the tetrad of chromatids.

Your Answer _____

_____

High-density lipoprotein (HDL) is called "good cholesterol," and can help remove excess cholesterol from blood vessels. (www.webmd.com)

Answers

A-53

(B)   In the first meiotic prophase, many events occur that provide the basis for variation even between offspring of the same parents.

First, the homologous chromosomes pair up in a process called synapsis. Since each homologous chromosome has already replicated, it exists as two sister chromatids joined together by a centromere. The paired chromosomes now exist as a tetrad of chromatids. Now crossing over, the exchange of segments between homologous non-sister chromatids, can occur. The site of cross-over is called a chiasma (*pl.* chiasmata). Since the chromosomes and later the chromatids will ultimately segregate randomly and independently, and since they contain recombined chromosome segments and, hence, recombined genetic traits, the foundation for variation is laid down.

Questions

Q-54

The cell organelles that are most similar to pro-karyotes are

(A) the mitochondria and chloroplasts.

(B) the rough and smooth endoplasmic reticula.

(C) the rough endoplasmic reticula and ribosomes.

(D) the rough endoplasmic reticula and Golgi apparatuses.

Your Answer _____

_____

It is estimated that in 2022, 5.13 billion retail prescriptions will be filled. (www.statista.com)

Answers

(A) A mitochondrion is a cellular organelle that utilizes oxygen to produce ATP. It has its own DNA, which replicates autonomously from the nuclear DNA. It is suspected, based on the size, structure, and biochemistry of mitochondria, that they were once prokaryotic cells similar to bacteria that formed a symbiotic relationship with a eukaryotic host. Due to evolution, the mitochondrion has lost its independence.

A similar story holds true for chloroplasts, which also have their own DNA, similar to that of bacteria. A chloroplast, with its capacity for photosynthesis, could have originally been an independent prokaryote, now dependent on the cell in which it lives.

The endoplasmic reticula (both rough and smooth), ribosomes, Golgi apparatus, and lysosomes do not contain their own DNA. Their functions are ultimately dictated by the nucleus. The ribosomes synthesize proteins. If the ribosomes are attached to the endoplasmic reticulum, making it rough endoplasmic reticulum, the proteins will enter the reticular lumen and be transported through the cell and reach the Golgi apparatus for modification and continued distribution. The smooth endoplasmic reticulum functions primarily in lipid synthesis.

Questions

Q–55

A phenotype refers to

(A) the genetic makeup of an individual.

(B) the expression of dominant traits.

(C) the expression of recessive traits.

(D) the manifest expression of the genotype.

Your Answer _____

Q–56

Heating a test-tube culture full of bacteria and killing them all is

(A) a density-dependent factor.

(B) an intrinsic factor.

(C) a result of exponential growth.

(D) None of the above

Your Answer _____

Answers

A–55

(D) The genotype is the actual genetic constitution of the individual, but the phenotype is the expression of those genes. For instance, the geno types that code for eye color are BB (homozygous dominant), Bb (heterozygous) and bb (homozygous recessive). There are thus three genotypes. But there are only two phenotypes: Bb and BB both code for brown eye color, as the allele for brown eyes (B) is dominant to that for blue eyes (b). Blue eyes are only possible with the genotype bb. (Note that green eyes are considered as blue, genotypically and phenotypically.) Thus a blue-eyed person knows his genotype immediately, but a brown-eyed person needs to look at his lineage to possibly figure out his genotype.

Phenotype includes all physical characteristics of an organism that are the results of genotype. A characteristic need not be seen by an observer to be included in an organism's phenotype (e.g., one's blood type is part of one's phenotype).

A–56

(D) In itself, the heat killing of the bacterial culture is unrelated to factors that regulate populations such as choices (A), (B), and (C). The decimation of this microbial population occurred when a critical environmental variable, in this case temperature, exceeded the range of tolerance that is characteristic of the species.

Questions

Q–57

All of the following are terms that describe viruses EXCEPT

(A) free-living.

(B) host-dependent.

(C) noncellular.

(D) protein and nucleic acid makeup.

Your Answer _____

_____

Q–58

Meiosis takes place in which of the following organs?

(A) Ovary

(B) Skeletal muscle of embryo

(C) Spleen

(D) Liver

Your Answer _____

_____

Answers

A–57

(A) Viruses are incredibly small (nanometers). They lack normal cellular structures and thus need a host organism to grow and reproduce. They consist of protein coats surrounding nucleic acid cores.

A–58

(A) Of all the organs mentioned, only the ovary is part of the reproductive system. Thus, meiosis would be expected to occur in some of the structures associated with the reproductive system. Choice (B) is part of the skeletal system while choices (C) and (D) are part of other body systems.

Questions

Q–59

What is the relationship, if any, between color blindness and hemophilia?

(A) Both are restricted to chromosomes coming from the father.

(B) Both are restricted to chromosomes coming from the mother.

(C) Both are sex-linked conditions.

(D) Both are caused by dominant genes.

Your Answer _____

_____

Q–60

Mutations are caused by

(A) base changes in DNA.

(B) base changes in RNA.

(C) changes in the sugars of DNA.

(D) changes in the phosphates of RNA.

Your Answer _____

_____

Answers

A–59

(C) Both are examples of sex-linked conditions carried by recessive genes on X-chromosomes.

A–60

(A) Mutations can be caused by changes in the nitrogenous bases of DNA. One change can be the replacement of one base pair for another within a segment of DNA. Other changes can be the insertion of extra base pairs, or the deletion of one or more base pairs. A change in RNA nucleotide sequence may result in faulty translation of a gene, but RNA is constantly degraded and synthesized; as long as DNA remains unchanged, RNA will almost always be correctly synthesized.

Questions

Q–61

What change in the normal structure of hemoglobin results in sickle-cell anemia?

(A) There is a change in the sequence of the amino acids.

(B) There is a substitution of one amino acid for another.

(C) There is a change in the number of nucleotides.

(D) The peptide bonds are broken in the sickle-cell hemoglobin molecule.

Your Answer _____

_____

Q–62

Fermentation

(A) results in the formation of lactic acid.

(B) does not require oxygen.

(C) does require oxygen.

(D) produces large amounts of energy.

Your Answer _____

_____

Answers

A-61

(B) The entire structural difference between a normal and a sickle-cell hemoglobin molecule consists of the substitution of the amino acid valine for the amino acid glutamic acid. This substitution occurs in the sixth position of each of the two B-chains in hemoglobin.

A-62

(B) Fermentation is the production of ethanol from glucose as done by yeast cells. In glycolysis, one glucose molecule is converted to two molecules of pyruvic acid and also provides enough energy for the synthesis of two molecules of ATP and two molecules of NADPH. The pyruvic acid, still containing much potential energy, can next enter either the anaerobic pathway or the aerobic pathway. In one type of anaerobic pathway, pyruvic acid is converted to ethanol by the action of yeast cells on sugar.

Questions

Q-63

Which of the following tissues is NOT related to connective tissue?

(A) Collagen

(B) Bone

(C) Cartilage

(D) Lymph

Your Answer _____

_____

Q-64

A respiratory system does not necessarily need

(A) an exchange surface with an adequate area.

(B) a means to transport gases to internal areas.

(C) a means of protecting exchange surfaces.

(D) a location deep inside an organism.

Your Answer _____

_____

Answers

A–63

(D) Connective tissue provides support for body parts and binds structures together. Options (B) and (C) are examples of connective tissue. Collagen (Option A) is a protein found in skin and bone, and is secreted by the cells of connective tissue. Collagen provides a rigid matrix in which connective tissue cells exist.

A–64

(D) Options (A) through (C) refer to characteristics of the respiratory system of both unicellular and multicellular organisms. In single-celled or simple organisms such as algae and flat worms, oxygen diffuses directly through cell membranes. Thus, location deep inside an organism is not a requirement of a respiratory system.

Questions

Q–65

T-cells are generally NOT involved in fighting

(A) cancer cells.

(B) transplanted foreign tissue.

(C) viral infections.

(D) bacterial infections.

Your Answer _____

_____

Q–66

Which statement about respiration is INCOR-RECT?

(A) Humans use positive-pressure breathing.

(B) When exhaling, the position of the diaphragm and ribs in humans is: ribs lowered, diaphragm raised.

(C) Abdominal breathing in humans does not depend on active transport of air.

(D) Frogs use positive-pressure breathing.

Your Answer _____

_____

Answers

A–65

(D) The primary targets of B-cells are bacterial infections. All other options are the targets of T-cells.

A–66

(A) Humans (mammals) and birds use negative pressure breathing whereby air is drawn into the lungs. This process involves the raising of the rib cage and the downward movement of the diaphragm during inhalation. The volume of the chest cavity is increased, reducing the internal air pressure, resulting in air being drawn into the lungs to equalize the pressure. In contrast, positive-pressure breathing occurs when air is **forced** into the lungs. For example, a frog closes its nostrils and raises the floor of its mouth, thus reducing the volume of the mouth cavity and forcing air into the lungs. Active transport of air does not occur in humans.

Questions

Q–67

In capillary exchange

(A)   proteins in the blood and tissue help to determine osmotic pressure.

(B)   osmotic pressure moves water outside the capillaries only.

(C)   blood pressure is greater than osmotic pressure at the venous end of the capillaries.

(D)   blood pressure is less than osmotic pressure at the arterial end of the capillaries.

Your Answer _____

_____

Q–68

A strand of DNA is a _____ and can generate a new _____ strand of DNA.

(A)   copy... identical

(B)   parent... identical

(C)   duplicate... duplicate

(D)   template... complementary

Your Answer _____

_____

Answers

A-67

(A) At the arterial end of the capillaries, the blood pressure is higher than the pressure of the tissue fluid outside the capillaries. This differential causes fluid to leave the capillaries and go into the tissue. At the same time the concentration of proteins in the tissue fluid is less than the concentration of proteins in the blood because the large protein molecules can not easily diffuse through the capillary walls. Thus, water tends to move into the capillaries by osmosis to equalize the osmotic pressure;this occurs at the venous end. Approximately 99% of the water that exits capillaries at the arterial ends due to the net force of blood pressure, re-enters the capillaries at their venous ends due to the net force of osmotic pressure.

A-68

(D) During self-replication, the DNA unwinds at the weak hydrogen bonds that join the complementary base pairs. Free nucleotides in the environment become attached to the open bases of the parent strands if the proper catalyzing enzymes are present. The attachments follow the principle of complementary base pairing so that the strand produced is complementary, not identical, to the intact parent strand. The original strand acts as a "template" for the generation of a complementary strand.

Questions

Q–69

Viruses have

(A) the ability to replicate their genetic material.

(B) the ability to make their own energy.

(C) their own metabolic machinery.

(D) their own enzymes.

Your Answer _____

_____

Q–70

Which condition is necessary for diffusion to occur?

(A) A living cell

(B) A permeable membrane

(C) A differentially permeable membrane

(D) A difference in concentration

Your Answer _____

_____

Answers

A-69

(A) Viruses are parasites in that they cannot multiply outside their host cell. They use the energy sources (option (B)), metabolic machinery (option (C)), and enzymes (option (D)) of the host cell. Viruses do have the ability to replicate their genetic material DNA or RNA. They do so by inserting a copy of their genetic material and using the resources of the host cell to replicate the material and to form their own protein coats. The virus particle then escapes from the host cell and is ready to infect another host cell.

A-70

(D) Diffusion occurs when there is a difference in the concentrations of substances and the goal is to have the particles distributed uniformly throughout. Diffusion can occur with or without a membrane (choices (B) and (C)). Lab experiments showing diffusion can be done with inanimate objects.

Questions

Q–71

Proteins are formed by combining

(A) lipids.

(B) monosaccharide and disaccharides.

(C) nucleic acids.

(D) amino acids.

Your Answer _____

_____

Q–72

An enzyme is a large organic molecule with a surface geometry that is composed of

(A) amino acids.

(B) monosaccharides.

(C) glycerol and fatty acids.

(D) polysaccharides.

Your Answer _____

_____

Answers

A-71

(D)　Proteins are composed of carbon, oxygen, hydrogen, nitrogen, and sometimes sulfur. These elements combine to form amino acids. Each amino acid has a carboxyl group (–COOH) and an amino group ($-NH_2$), which are attached to a carbon atom. In addition, side groups (called radicals) are also attached to the carbon atom. There are 20 different kinds of amino acids, each with a different side group.

A-72

(A)　An enzyme is a type of protein that catalyzes biological reactions. The surface geometry plays an important part in its specificity for substance molecules.

Questions

Q–73

Enzymes

(A) are highly sensitive to pH charges.

(B) are highly specific to the reactions they catalyze.

(C) work best at optimum temperatures.

(D) All of the above

Your Answer _____

_____

Q–74

Which is a characteristic of a hormone?

(A) They are produced in the tissue that they affect.

(B) Small quantities can produce effects.

(C) They work interdependently with other hormones.

(D) Both (B) and (C)

Your Answer _____

_____

Answers

A–73

(D) Enzymes require specific conditions of temperature, pH, and substrate under which they operate at maximum efficiency. In humans, enzymes work best at an optimum temperature of 98.6° F, 37° C, but at various pH values, dependent on the enzyme, the substrate, and the location of reaction.

A–74

(D) Choice (A) is incorrect. Hormones of animals are produced in certain tissues but are transported to and affect other tissues. They can exert specific influences using very small quantities.

Questions

Q–75

The formation of eggs and sperm is called

(A) gametogenesis.

(B) gastrulation.

(C) ovulation.

(D) fertilization.

Your Answer _____

_____

Answers

A–75

(A) The sperm and the egg form within the parental reproductive system. The sperm grows a tail that will help it move to the egg cell, and the egg cytoplasm gains nutrients.

Take Quiz 1 at the REA Study Center to test your immediate grasp of the topics in this section.
(www.rea.com/studycenter)

Section II
Chemical Processes

DIRECTIONS: Each of the questions or incomplete statements in this section is followed by four suggested answers or completions. Select the one that is best in each case.

Questions

Q–1

The element with atomic number 32 (see page 472) describes

(A) a metal.

(B) a nonmetal.

(C) a metalloid.

(D) a halogen.

Your Answer _____

Q–2

The electronic configuration of N_2 is correctly represented as

(A) : N : N :

(B) : N : : N

(C) : N : : N :

(D) : N : : : N :

Your Answer _____

Answers

A–1

(C)   Referring to the periodic table we see that element 32 is germanium. Germanium is a metalloid as are boron, silicon, arsenic, antimony, tellurium, polonium, and astatine. Chemically, metalloids exhibit both positive and negative oxidation states and combine with metals and nonmetals. They are characterized by approximately half-filled outer electron shells and electronegativity values between those of the metals and the nonmetals.

A–2

(D)   The prime consideration in representing the bonding of a poly atomic element or compound is that each atom bonded should have a complete valence shell (eight electrons except hydrogen and helium which have two). Since nitrogen is in Group VA it has five valence electrons illustrated as

$: \overset{\cdot}{N} \cdot$

Diatomic nitrogen must have the structure

$: N ::: N :$ (or $: N \equiv N :$)

to completely fill the valence shells of both atoms.

Questions

Q-3

All of the following are chemical changes EXCEPT

(A) dissolving NaCl in water.

(B) burning a piece of wood.

(C) ozone absorbing ultraviolet light.

(D) dissolving Na metal in water.

Your Answer _____

_____

Q-4

The greatest reduction of kinetic activity of water molecules occurs when water is

(A) cooled as a solid.

(B) cooled as a liquid.

(C) converted from a liquid to a gas.

(D) converted from a gas to a liquid.

Your Answer _____

_____

Answers

A–3

(A) Dissolving sodium chloride in water is an example of a physical change. A physical change alters the physical properties of a substance while maintaining its composition. If the water solution of NaCl were to be evaporated we would once again have solid sodium chloride. Chemical changes involve altering the composition and structure of a substance and are always associated with changes in energy. Wood and oxygen are changed to CO_2, H_2O and nitrogen oxides while ozone is changed to diatomic oxygen and sodium and water are changed to sodium hydroxide and hydrogen gas.

A–4

(D) Molecules in the gaseous state have the greatest kinetic activity. The difference in energy between the liquid and gas phases is greater than the difference in energy between the solid and liquid phases. This may be readily seen by the energy changes occurring in water; the heat of fusion of water is 80 calories/gram, while the heat of vaporization is 540 calories/gram.

Questions

Q–5

The extremely high melting point of diamond (carbon) may be explained by large numbers of

(A) covalent bonds.

(B) ionic bonds.

(C) hydrogen bonds.

(D) van der Waals forces.

Your Answer _____

_____

$H_2 SO_4^{-2}$

-8

Q–6

The oxidation number of sulfur in $Na\overset{+}{H}\overset{+}{S}O_4^{-2}$ is

(A)   0.

(B) +2.

(C) –2.

(D) +6.

Your Answer _____

_____

Answers

A-5

(A) Diamond, composed solely of carbon, cannot have ionic bonds or hydrogen bonds. Van der Waals attraction between the nucleus of one atom and the electrons of an adjacent atom are relatively weak compared to the covalent bonding network (sp^3 hybrid) between the carbon atoms in diamond. On the other hand, graphite (another allotropic form of carbon) is sp^2 hybrid and not strongly bonded as compared to diamond.

A-6

(D) The oxidation state of sulfur in sodium bisulfate may be determined by recalling that the oxidation states of sodium, hydrogen, and oxygen are usually +1, +1, and –2, respectively. Since the sum of the oxidation states for the atoms of a neutral compound are zero we have:

oxidation state of S + 1 + 1 + 4(–2) = 0

∴ oxidation state of S = +6

So, the oxidation number of sulfur in $NaHSO_4$ is +6.

Questions

Q-7

The action of perchloric acid with barium hydroxide is

(A) an elimination reaction.

(B) a neutralization reaction.

(C) an oxidation-reduction reaction.

(D) a hydrolysis reaction.

Your Answer _____

_____

Q-8

The transition metals are characterized by

(A) completely filled d subshells.

(B) completely filled f subshells.

(C) partially filled d subshells.

(D) Both (A) and (C) are correct.

Your Answer _____

_____

Answers

A-7

(D) This is an example of a neutralization reaction, in which an acid and a base react to produce water and a salt. It is not a redox reaction, since barium maintains an oxidation number of +2 throughout. An elimination reaction is a type of organic reaction. Hydrolysis involves water breaking covalent bonds.

A-8

(D) The transition metals may have either completely filled or partially filled, but not empty, sub shells (3d, 4d, and 5d). Lanthanides and actinides are characterized by the electrons in the 4f and 5f sub shells, respectively.

Questions

Q–9

An equilibrium reaction may be forced to completion by

(A) adding a catalyst.

(B) increasing the pressure.

(C) increasing the temperature.

(D) removing the products from the reaction mixture as they are formed.

Your Answer _____

_____

Slightly more than half (55%) of full-time chain pharmacists are male. (www.nacds.org)

Answers

(D)   Le Chatelier's Principle may be used to predict equilibrium reactions: If a stress is placed on a system in equilibrium, the equilibrium shifts so as to counteract that stress. Hence, increasing the reactant concentration favors formation of the products while decreasing the reactant concentration favors formation of the reactants. The same holds true for altering the product concentrations. Increasing the temperature favors the reaction that absorbs heat while decreasing the temperature favors the reaction that releases heat. Increasing the pressure favors the reaction that decreases the volume of a closed system while decreasing the pressure favors the reaction resulting in an increased volume (moles of gaseous product produced are the only things counted since liquids and solids occupy a relatively small volume in comparison). However, temperature and pressure dependencies cannot be inferred from this question. The addition of a catalyst alters the reaction rate but not the position of equilibrium. The only way completion can be obtained is to remove the products as they are formed. Now the state of the reaction becomes non equilibrium, but it tries to come in equilibrium state once again. This leads to formation of more products, which in turn leads to completion of the given reaction.

Questions

Q-10

Which of the following salts will result in a basic solution when dissolved in water?

(A) $Ba(NO_3)_2$

(B) Na_2S

(C) $Al_2(SO_4)_3$

(D) $Pb_3(PO_4)_2$

Your Answer _____

_____

$$H_2O + \underline{} \rightarrow H\underline{} + \underline{}OH$$

Successful completion of the academic and clinical requirements of a graduate degree from an accredited program, passage of a state board examination, and a period internship under the guidance of a licensed pharmacist are all required in order to obtain a license to practice pharmacy.

Answers

(B) The salts of strong bases and weak acids hydrolyze to form a basic solution, while the salts of weak bases and strong acids hydrolyze to form an acidic solution.

$$Ba(NO_3)_2 + 2H_2O \rightarrow 2HNO_3 + Ba(OH)_2$$

A neutral solution is produced since both nitric acid and barium hydroxide are completely dissociated and each is present in the same concentration (barium hydroxide has 2 hydroxy groups)

$$Na_2S + 2H_2O \rightarrow H_2S + 2NaOH$$

A basic solution is produced since hydrosulfuric acid is a weak acid and sodium hydroxide is a strong base.

$$Al_2(SO_4)_3 + 6H_2O \rightarrow 3H_2SO_4 + 2Al(OH)_3$$

An acidic solution is produced since aluminum hydroxide is insoluble and sulfuric acid is a strong acid.

$$Pb_3(PO_4)_2 + 6H_2O \rightarrow 2H_3PO_4 + 3Pb(OH)_2$$

An acidic solution is produced since phosphoric acid is a weak acid and lead (II) hydroxide is insoluble.

$$NaCl + H_2O \rightarrow HCl + NaOH$$

A neutral solution is produced since hydrochloric acid is a strong acid and sodium hydroxide is a strong base.

Questions

Q-11

The radioactive decay of plutonium −238(Pu) produces an alpha particle and a new atom. That new atom is

(A) $^{234}_{92}$Pu.

(B) $^{234}_{92}$Cm.

(C) $^{234}_{92}$U.

(D) $^{242}_{96}$Cm.

Your Answer _____

_____

Answers

A–11

(C) Plutonium-238 has a mass of 238 and an atomic number of 94. The atomic mass tells us the number of protons and neutrons in the nucleus, while the atomic number tells us the number of protons. An alpha particle $\binom{4}{2}\alpha$ is a helium nucleus composed of 2 neutrons and 2 protons (atomic mass of 4). Hence, upon emission of an alpha particle, the atomic number decreases by 2 and the atomic mass decreases by 4. This gives us $^{234}_{92}X$. Examining the periodic table we find that element 92 is uranium. Thus, our new atom is $^{234}_{92}U$. $^{234}_{92}Pu$ and $^{234}_{92}Cm$ are impossible since the atomic number of plutonium is 94 and that of curium is 96. $^{242}_{96}Pu$ and $^{242}_{96}Cm$ are impossible since these nuclei could only be produced by fusion of $^{238}_{94}Pu$ with an alpha particle. In addition, $^{242}_{96}Pu$ is incorrectly named.

∴ The reaction (decay) is $_{94}Pu^{238} \rightarrow {}_{92}U^{234} + 2^{\alpha 4}$

Questions

Q–12

What is the approximate melting point of 0.2 liters of water containing 6.20g of ethylene glycol ($C_2H_6O_2$)?

(A) $-1.86°C$

(B) $-0.93°C$

(C) $0°C$

(D) $0.93°C$

Your Answer _____

① find moles (need MW)

② find molality ($\frac{mol}{kg}$) ← convert g to kg

The first professional pharmacies are said to have been in Baghdad in the 13th century. (www.who2.com)

Answers

(B) First, we determine the number of moles present in solution taking the molecular weight of ethylene glycol to be 62g. Thus,

$$6.20g \times \frac{1 \, mole}{62g} = 0.1 \, mole \, of \, ethylene \, glycol$$

We must also know the molality—the ratio of moles of solute to kilograms of solvent. The number of kilograms of solvent is

$$0.2l \times \frac{1 \, kg}{1l} = 0.2 \, kg$$

since the density of water is 1g/ml. The molality of the solution is

$$\frac{0.1 \, mole}{0.2 \, kg} = 0.5 \, molal.$$

For H_2O, the molal freezing point depression constant is 1.86°C/molal. Thus, the freezing point depression is

$$0.5 \, molal \times \frac{1.86°C}{molal} = 0.93°C$$

Thus, the melting point would be
$$0°C - 0.93°C = -0.93°C$$

Questions

Q–13

What is the molecular formula of a compound composed of 25.9% nitrogen and 74.1% oxygen by mass?

(A) NO

(B) NO_2

(C) N_2O

(D) N_2O_5

Your Answer $N = 14.5 \quad O = 13.6$

$N = 15 \quad O = 16$

$30 \quad 80$

$$\left(\frac{2\,moles}{1L}\right)\left(\frac{1L}{1,000mL}\right)\left(\frac{200mL}{1}\right) = \frac{400}{1,000}$$

Q–14

How many moles of sulfate ion are in 200 ml of a $2M$ sodium sulfate solution?

(A) 0.2 mole

(B) 0.4 mole

(C) 0.6 mole

(D) 0.8 mole

Your Answer _____

_____

Answers

A–13

(D) A 100g sample of this gas contains 25.9g of nitrogen and 74.1g of oxygen. Dividing each of these weights by their respective atomic weights gives us the molar ratio of N to O for the gas. This gives

$$N_{\frac{25.9}{14}} O_{\frac{74.1}{16}} = N_{1.85} O_{4.63}$$

Dividing both subscripts by the smallest subscript gives

$$N_{\frac{1.85}{1.85}} O_{\frac{4.63}{1.85}} = N_1 O_{2.5}$$

Doubling both subscripts so as to have whole numbers gives us N_2O_5.

A–14

(B) A $1M$ sodium sulfate (Na_2SO_4) solution contains one mole of sulfate ion per liter of solution. Thus 0.2L of a $1M$ solution contains 0.2 mole of sulfate ion. 0.2L of a $2M$ solution would then contain 0.4 mole of sulfate ion.

Questions

Q–15

What volume of water is required to produce 5 liters of oxygen by the process below?

$$2 H_2O_{(g)} \rightarrow 2 H_{2(g)} + O_{2(g)}$$

(A) 3 liters

(B) 5 liters

(C) 10 liters

(D) 14 liters

Your Answer _____

---

① Balence Equ.

Q–16

The structure of the third member of the alkyne series is

(A) $H - C \equiv C - H$.

(B) $H - C \equiv C - CH_3$.

(C) $H - C \equiv C - CH_2 - CH_3$.

(D) $H - C \equiv C - C \equiv C - H$.

Your Answer _____

Answers

A–15

(C) Balancing the reaction equation gives

$$2H_2O \rightarrow 2H_2 + O_2$$

As may be seen from the equation, two units of water react to produce one unit of oxygen. Thus 10L of water are required to produce 5L of oxygen.

A–16

(C) The first member of the alkyne series is acetylene (or ethyne), whose structure is

$$HC \equiv CH$$

The second is propyne: $HC \equiv C - CH_3$
The third is butyne: $HC \equiv C - CH_2 - CH_3$
Note that there are no analogous compounds in the alkene or alkyne series for the first member of the alkane series (methane – CH_4).

Questions

Q–17

Sodium chloride (NaCl) would be most soluble in

P

(A) ether. NP

(B) benzene. NP

(C) water. P

(D) carbon tetrachloride. NP

Your Answer _____

Q–18

$Na\overset{\ominus}{C}OCH_3$

Hydrolysis of sodium acetate yields

(A) a strong acid and a strong base.

(B) a weak acid and a weak base.

(C) a strong acid and a weak base.

(D) a weak acid and a strong base.

Your Answer _____ NaOH is a strong base _____

111

Answers

(C)   Polar solutes such as sodium chloride are more soluble in polar solvents than in non-polar solvents and non-polar solutes are more soluble in non-polar solvents (like dissolves like). Water is the only polar solvent given.

(D)   The hydrolysis reaction for sodium acetate proceeds as follows:

$$CH_3\overset{\displaystyle O}{\overset{\|}{C}}ONa + H_2O \rightarrow CH_3\overset{\displaystyle O}{\overset{\|}{C}}OH + \boxed{NaOH}$$

The products of the reaction are a weak acid (acetic acid) and a strong base (sodium hydroxide).

Questions

Q-19

How many moles of electrons must be removed from 0.5 mole of Fe^{2+} to produce Fe^{3+}?

(A) 0.5

(B) 1.0

(C) 1.5

(D) 2.0

Your Answer _____

Q-20

What is the pH of a $0.01M$ NaOH solution?

(A) 4

(B) 7

(D) 12

$$pH = -\log[H^+]$$

Your Answer _____

Answers

A–19

(A) Iron loses 1 mole of electrons when one mole of Fe^{2+} reacts to produce Fe^{3+}. The removal of 0.5 mole of electrons is required to oxidize iron from the +2 to the +3 state.

A–20

(D) The pH of a solution is defined as
$$pH = -log[H^+]$$
We are not given the $[H^+]$ however. There are two ways of solving this problem. The first relies on the fact that:
$$K_w = [H^+][OH^-] = 1 \times 10^{-14}$$
Rearranging gives

$$[H^+] = \frac{K_w}{[OH^-]} = \frac{1 \times 10^{-14}}{1 \times 10^{-2}} = 1 \times 10^{-12}$$

and $\qquad pH = -log\ 1 \times 10^{-12} = 12$
Alternatively, we define pOH as
$$pOH = -log[OH^-]$$
which gives
$$pOH = -log\ 1 \times 10^{-2} = 2.$$
Recalling that $pH + pOH = 14$ we have upon rearrangement:
$$pH = 14 - pOH = 12$$

Questions

Q-21

Twenty liters of NO gas react with excess oxygen. How many liters of NO_2 gas are produced if the NO gas reacts completely?

(A) 5 liters

(B) 10 liters

(C) 20 liters

(D) 40 liters

$$NO + \tfrac{1}{2}O_2 \rightarrow NO_2$$

$$2NO + 10O_2 \rightarrow 20NO_2$$

Your Answer Balence Equ.

Q-22

What is the molar concentration of I^- in 1 liter of a saturated water solution of PbI_2 if the K_{sp} of lead iodide is 1.4×10^{-8}?

(A) 3.0×10^{-3}

(B) 1.2×10^{-4}

(C) 5.9×10^{-5}

(D) 2.4×10^{-3}

Math!

Your Answer _____

Answers

A-21

(C) The reaction in question is
$$NO + \tfrac{1}{2}O_2 \rightarrow NO_2$$
or using the given coefficients
$$20NO + 10O_2 \rightarrow 20NO_2$$
Note that the unit of the coefficients used is liters, not moles. This does not affect the calculation since moles and liters are directly related in the case of gases (1 mole of a gas occupies 22.4 liters at STP).

A-22

(A) The solubility product of lead (II) iodide is given by
$$K_{sp} = [Pb^{2+}] [I^-]^2$$
where $[Pb^{2+}]$ and $[I^-]$ are the concentrations of lead ion and iodide in solution, respectively. We know that $K_{sp} = 1.4 \times 10^{-8}$ and that the concentration of iodide in solution is twice that of the lead ion from the dissociation:

given

$$PbI_2 \rightarrow Pb^{2+} + 2I^-$$
Setting $[Pb^{2+}] = x$, we know that $[I^-] = 2x$. Thus,
$$K_{sp} = [Pb^{2+}] [I^-]^2 = (x)(2x)2 = 1.4 \times 10^{-8}.$$
Solving for x gives
$$4x^3 = 1.4 \times 10^{-8}$$
and $x = 1.5 \times 10^{-3}$
Recalling that $[I^-] = 2x$ we have
$$[I^-] = 2(1.5 \times 10^{-3}) = 3 \times 10^{-3}$$

Questions

Q–23

A 0.5 molal solution could be prepared by dissolving 20g of NaOH in

(A) 0.5 liter of water.

(B) 1 liter of water.

(C) 0.5 kg of water.

(D) 1 kg of water.

Your Answer _____

① find moles

$$\frac{0.5 \text{ moles}}{1 \text{ kg}}$$

Famous people who spent time behind the pharmacy counter include the following: Dante, Isaac Newton, O. Henry, Henrik Ibsen, Hubert H. Humphrey, Benedict Arnold. (www.who2.com)

Answers

(D)　　The molality of a solution (m) is defined as the number of moles of solute dissolved in one kilogram of solvent. The number of moles of NaOH to be used is determined to be:

$$20g \text{ of NaOH} \times \frac{1 \text{ mole of NaOH}}{40g \text{ of NaOH}}$$

$$= 0.5 \text{ moles of NaOH}$$

Thus:

$$0.5m = \frac{0.5 \text{ mole of NaOH}}{x \text{ kilograms of water}}$$

Rearranging:

$$x = \frac{0.5}{0.5} = 1 \text{ kg of water}$$

Questions

Q–24

The equilibrium expression, $K_e = [CO_2]$ represents the reaction

(A) $C_{(s)} + O_{2(g)} \rightleftharpoons CO_{2(g)}$.

(B) $CO_{(g)} + \frac{1}{2}O_{2(g)} \rightleftharpoons CO_{2(g)}$.

(C) $CaCO_{3(s)} \rightleftharpoons CaO_{(s)} + CO_{2(g)}$.

(D) $CO_{2(g)} \rightleftharpoons C_{(s)} + O_{2(g)}$.

Your Answer ___ K_e only includes gases!

Aspirin went on sale as the first pharmaceutical drug in 1899, after Felix Hoffman, a German chemist at the drug company Bayer, successfully modified Salicylic Acid, a compound found in willow bark. (www.corsinet.com)

Answers

A–24

(C) The equilibrium constant is defined as the product of the concentrations of the gaseous products raised to the power of their coefficients, divided by the product of the gaseous reactant concentrations raised to the power of their coefficients. Only gaseous reactants and products are included in K_e since the concentrations of liquids and solids participating in the reaction are assumed to be large (as compared to those of the gases) and relatively constant. The expressions of the equilibrium constants for the reactions given are:

(A) $K_e = \dfrac{[CO_2]}{[O_2]}$

(B) $K_e = \dfrac{[CO_2]}{[CO][O_2]^{1/2}}$

(C) $K_e = [CO_2]$

(D) $K_e = \dfrac{[O_2]}{[CO_2]}$

Questions

Q–25

The following reaction coordinates cannot be associated with

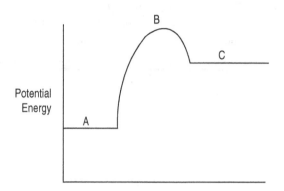

(A)   an endothermic reaction from A to C.

(B)   an exothermic reaction from A to C.

(C)   the activation energy for the reaction.

(D)   the energy for the intermediate.

Your Answer _____

_____

1900: Bayer Aspirin was the first drug ever to be marketed in tablet form. (www.corsinet.com)

Answers

A–25

(B) Heat was absorbed by the system during the reaction as indicated by the products having a greater potential energy than the reactants. A reaction in which heat is absorbed in order to produce the products is said to be endothermic.

The United States Pharmacopeia (USP) is the official public standards-setting authority for all prescription and over-the-counter medicines, dietary supplements, and other healthcare products manufactured and sold in the United States. (www.usp.org)

Questions

Q–26

The primary products of hydrocarbon combustion are

(A) water and carbon.

(B) water and carbon monoxide.

(C) water and carbon dioxide.

(D) hydrogen and carbon monoxide.

Your Answer _____

_____

Q–27

How many moles of CO_2 are represented by 1.8×10^{24} atoms?

(A) 1

(B) 2

(C) 3

(D) 4

Your Answer _____

_____

Answers

A–26

(C) Water and carbon dioxide are the primary products of hydrocarbon combustion. These are the only products in the case of complete combustion. For example,

$$C_2H_6 + \frac{7}{2}O_2 \rightarrow 2\,CO_2 + 3H_2O$$

A–27

(A) By simple unit conversion:

$$1.8 \times 10^{24}\ atoms\ \times \frac{1\ mole}{6.02 \times 10^{23}\ molecules}$$

$$\times\ \frac{1\ molecule}{3\ atoms} = 1\ mole$$

since each CO_2 molecule is composed of three atoms.

Questions

Q-28

Which of the following is responsible for the abnormally high boiling point of water?

(A) Covalent bonding

(B) Hydrogen bonding

(C) High polarity

(D) Large dielectric constant

Your Answer _____

_____

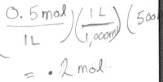

$23 + 35$
$= 58 g/mol \cdot \cancel{500}$
NaCl

Q-29

About how many grams of sodium chloride would be dissolved in water to form a 0.5 M solution in 500 ml of solution?

(A) 7

(B) 29

(C) 14.5

(D) 58

$$\left(\frac{0.5\,mol}{1\,L}\right)\left(\frac{1\,L}{1,000\,ml}\right)(500\,ml)$$

$$= .2\,mol$$

K
H
D
U
D
C
m

Your Answer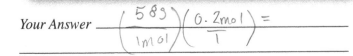

$$\left(\frac{58g}{1\,mol}\right)\left(\frac{0.2\,mol}{1}\right) =$$

Answers

A–28

(B) Hydrogen bonding between molecules increases their stability and thus increases the boiling point of water.

A–29

(C) The formula weight of *NaCl* is about 58 grams, which forms a 1 M solution in 1000 ml of solution. 29 grams forms a 0.5 M solution in 1000 ml. In 500 ml, 14.5, or half this amount, is needed.

Questions

Q–30

Which of the following is true of an electrochemical cell?

(A) The cell voltage is independent of concentration.

(B) The anode is negatively charged.

(C) The cathode is the site of reduction.

(D) Charge is carried from one electrode to the other by metal atoms passing through the solution.

Your Answer _____

Q–31

An element of atomic number 17 has an atomic weight of 37. How many neutrons are in its nucleus?

(A) 17

(B) 18

(C) 20

(D) 37

$$37 \ A.W.$$
$$-17 \ A.\#.$$
$$\overline{20}$$

Your Answer _____

Answers

Red Cat   An Ox

A–30

(C) The cathode of an electrochemical cell is defined as the site of reduction and the anode is defined as the site of oxidation.

GEB   LEO

A–31

(C) The atomic number gives the number of protons in the nucleus and the atomic weight gives the sum of the number of protons and neutrons. Thus, the number of neutrons is given by the difference between the atomic number and the atomic weight.

Questions

Q–32

The most probable oxidation number of an element with an atomic number of 53 is

(A) −5.

(B) −1.

(C) +1.

(D) +5.

Your Answer _____

_____

Q–33

What is the concentration of $[OH^-]$ in a NH_4OH solution if it has a pH of 11?

(A) 10^{-1}

(B) 10^{-3}

(C) 10^{-5}

(D) 10^{-9}

1×10^{-11}

1×10^{-3}

$= 1 \times 10^{-14}$

Your Answer _____

_____

Answers

A-32

(B) Element 53 is iodine, a member of the halogens (Group VIIA). The halogens usually have an oxidation number of –1 although some other values sometimes (rarely) occur.

A-33

(B) A solution of pH 11 has $[H^+] = 1 \times 10^{-11}$ by the equation $pH = -log[H^+]$. Recalling that $K_w = [H^+][OH^-] = 10^{-14}$ we have

$$[OH^-] = \frac{K_w}{[H^+]} = \frac{10^{-14}}{[H^+]} = \frac{10^{-14}}{10^{-11}} = 10^{-3}$$

Questions

20 ml of NaOH is needed to titrate 30 ml of a 6M HCl solution. The molarity of the NaOH is

(A) 1M.

(B) 3M.

(C) 6M.

(D) 9M.

Your Answer _____

_____

$$20(x) = (30)(6)$$
$$20x = 180$$
$$x = 9$$

More than 100 years ago, the felt hat makers of England used mercury to stabilize wool. Most of them eventually became poisoned by the fumes, as demonstrated by the Mad Hatter in Lewis Carroll's Alice in Wonderland. *(www.corsinet.com)*

Answers

(D)   Using the formula $M_1V_1 = M_2V_2$ and rearranging we obtain

$$M_2 = \frac{M_1V_1}{V_2} = \frac{(6M)(30ml)}{20ml} = 9M\ NaOH$$

Questions

This method is best suited for producing and collecting a gas that is

Litmus
Solution
of Hypo

(A) lighter than air.

(B) heavier than air.

(C) soluble in water.

(D) nonsoluble in water.

Your Answer _____

_____

Answers

A–35

(B)   This setup is used to prepare gases such as Cl_2 and HCl, which are heavier than air.

ASHP is the 30,000-member national professional association that represents pharmacists who practice in hospitals, health maintenance organizations, long-term care facilities, home care, and other components of health care systems. (www.ashp.org)

Questions

Q–36

How many grams of water can be produced when 8g of hydrogen reacts with 8g of oxygen?

(A) 8g

(B) 9g

(C) 18g

(D) 27g

Your Answer _limiting reagent_

$2H_2 + O_2 \rightarrow 2H_2O$

Q–37

The relation $P_1V_1 = P_2V_2$ is known as

(A) Boyle's Law.

(B) Charles's Law.

(C) van der Waals' Law.

(D) the combined gas law.

Your Answer _____

Answers

A–36

(B) The reaction in question is
$$2H_2 + O_2 \rightarrow 2H_2O$$
Converting the given quantities to moles:
$$8g \text{ of } H_2 \times \frac{1 \text{ mole of } H_2}{2g \text{ of } H_2} = 4 \text{ moles of } H_2$$

$$8g \text{ of } O_2 \times \frac{1 \text{ mole of } O_2}{32g \text{ of } O_2} = 0.25 \text{ moles of } O_2$$

Oxygen is the limiting reactant in this reaction. Multiplying all coefficients by 0.25 in order to obtain 0.25 O_2 we have
$$0.5H_2 + 0.25O_2 \rightarrow 0.5H_2O$$
Converting to grams:
$$0.5 \text{ mole of } H_2O \times \frac{18g \text{ of } H_2O}{1 \text{ mole of } H_2O} = 9g \text{ of } H_2O$$

A–37

(A) Boyle's Law shows that the volume of a gas varies inversely with the pressure at constant temperature.

Questions

Q–38

Which of the following indicates a basic solution?

(A) $[H^+] > 10^{-7}$

(B) $[H^+] > 10^{-10}$

(C) pH = 5

(D) pH = 9

Your Answer _____

_____

Q–39

Amphoteric substances are best described as

(A) having the same number of protons and electrons but different numbers of neutrons.

(B) having the same composition but occurring in different molecular structures.

(C) being without definite shape.

(D) having both acid and base properties.

Your Answer _____

_____

Answers

A–38

(D)   A basic (alkaline) solution is indicated by a hydronium ion concentration less than 10^{-7} or identically, $pH > 7$ since $pH = -log[H^+]$. A solution with $[H^+] > 10^{-10}$ may be basic ($10^{-10} < [H^+] < 10^{-7}$) or acidic ($[H^+] > 10^{-7}$).

A–39

(D)   An amphoteric substance has both acid and base properties. Isotopes of an element have the same number of protons and electrons but different numbers of neutrons.① Isomers of a compound are indicated by the same molecular formulas but different structures.② Amorphous substances are designated as having no definite shape.③ Allotropes of a substance have the same composition but have different crystalline structures.④

①   (for example, $^{12}_{6}C$ and $^{13}_{6}C$)
②   (for example, 1-propanol and 2-propanol)
③   (for example, the product obtained when liquid sulfur is poured in water)
④   (for example, rhombic and monoclinic sulfur)

Questions

Q-40

The Fahrenheit temperature corresponding to 303K is

(A) −15°.

(B) 22°.

(C) 49°.

(D) 86°.

Your Answer _____

_____

$80 g/mol$

Q-41

What is the density of bromine vapor at STP?

(A) 2.5g/liter

(B) 2.9g/liter

(C) 3.6g/liter

(D) 7.1g/liter

Your Answer _____

guessed
but
the 1st
guess
was
correct!

DONT
DOUBT

Answers

(D) Converting to the Celsius scale ($t = T - 273$)
we have

$$t = 303 - 273 = 30°C$$

Converting to the Fahrenheit scale:

$$°F = \frac{9}{5}(°C) + 32$$

$$°F = \frac{9}{5}(30) + 32$$

$$°F = 86$$

A–41

(D) Since the volume of one mole of an ideal gas is 22.4 liters, we have

$$\frac{160g \text{ of } Br_2}{1 \text{ mole of } Br_2} \times \frac{1 \text{ mole of } Br_2}{22.4 \text{ liters}} = \frac{7.1g \text{ of } Br_2}{\text{liter}}$$

Questions

Q–42

The yield of $AB_{(g)}$

$$A_{(g)} + B_{(g)} \rightleftharpoons AB_{(g)} + heat$$

would be increased by

(A) decreasing the pressure.

(B) adding additional AB to the reaction mixture.

(C) decreasing the temperature.

(D) adding a nonreactive liquid to the reaction mixture.

Your Answer _____

_____

"Soldiers disease" is a term for morphine addiction. The Civil War produced over 400,000 morphine addicts. (www.corsinet. com)

Answers

(C) According to Le Chatelier's Principle, if a stress is placed on an equilibrium system, the equilibrium is shifted in the direction, which reduces the effect of that stress. This stress may be in the form of changes in pressure, temperature, concentrations, etc. By decreasing the pressure on the system, the system shifts in a direction so as to increase the pressure. For our reaction, the reverse reaction rate would increase since a larger volume (hence a greater pressure) results. This is due to the fact that two moles of gaseous product will result as opposed to one mole if the forward reaction were favored. Note that only gaseous products are accounted for when considering pressure effects. Adding AB to the reaction mixture would also serve to favor the reverse reaction since the system reacts to this stress by producing more A and B. Decreasing the temperature favors the forward reaction since heat (which will counteract the stress by increasing the temperature) is liberated in this process. The addition of a nonreactive liquid to the reaction mixture has no effect on the reaction rates (assuming pressure and temperature to remain constant). Decreasing the volume of the reaction mixture has the same effect as increasing the pressure (Boyle's Law) if the temperature is constant.

Questions

The functional group shown below represents

$$
\begin{array}{c}
O \\
\parallel \\
R - C - H
\end{array}
$$

(A) an alcohol.

(B) an ether.

(C) an aldehyde.

(D) a ketone.

Your Answer _____

_____

Answers

Need to Know!

(C) The functional group of an alcohol is indicated by

R – OH;

that of an ether is

R – O – R^1;

an aldehyde is indicated by

$$
\begin{array}{c}
O \\
\parallel \\
R - C - H;
\end{array}
$$

while that of a ketone is

$$
\begin{array}{c}
O \\
\parallel \\
R - C - R^1
\end{array}
$$

Derivatives of organic acids; esters, amides, and acid anhydrides for example, have the following functional groups:

carboxylic acid

$$
\begin{array}{c}
O \\
\parallel \\
R - C - OH
\end{array}
$$

ester

$$
\begin{array}{c}
O \\
\parallel \\
R - C - O - R^1
\end{array}
$$

amide

$$
\begin{array}{c}
O \\
\parallel \\
R - C - NH_2
\end{array}
$$

acid anhydride

$$
\begin{array}{cc}
O & O \\
\parallel & \parallel \\
R - C - O - C - R^1
\end{array}
$$

Questions

Q–44

What is the molarity of a 10 ml solution in which 3.7g of KCl are dissolved?

(A) 0.05*M*

(B) 0.1*M*

(C) 1*M*

(D) 5*M*

Your Answer _____

_____

$00\ 3.7g$ $10mL$ 39
$\qquad\qquad\qquad\qquad\qquad\qquad +35$
$\qquad\qquad\qquad\qquad\qquad\qquad\overline{74}$

$.0037kg$ $010.$

$.0037kg$ $.01L$ $\dfrac{3.7}{74} = 0.05$

$\left(3.7g\right)\left(\dfrac{1mol}{74g}\right)$

Q–45

Isomers differ in

(A) the number of neutrons in their nuclei.

(B) their atomic compositions.

(C) their molecular weights. ← *isotopes*

(D) their molecular structures.

Your Answer _____

_____

Answers

A–44

(D) Converting to moles:

$$3.7g \text{ of } KCl \times \frac{1 \text{ mole of } KCl}{74g \text{ of } KCl} = 0.05 \text{ mole of } KCl$$

Converting to liters of solution:

$$10 \text{ } ml \times \frac{1 \text{ liter}}{1,000 \text{ } ml} = 0.01 \text{ liter of solution}$$

Molarity is defined as the number of moles of solute dissolved in one liter of solution. Thus,

$$M = \frac{0.05 \text{ mole of } KCl}{0.01 \text{ liter of solution}}$$

A–45

(D) Isomers differ only in their molecular structures. Isotopes vary in the number of neutrons in the nucleus and thus have different weights.

Questions

Q–46

Which of the following indicates the functional group of an ether?

(A) R — OH

(B) R — O — R¹

(C)
$$R - \overset{\overset{\displaystyle O}{\|}}{C} - H$$

(D)
$$R - \overset{\overset{\displaystyle O}{\|}}{C} - R^1$$

Your Answer _____

_____

Q–47

The equilibrium expression, $K = [Ag^+][Cl^-]$ describes the reaction

(A) $AgCl \rightarrow Ag^+ + Cl^-$.

(B) $Ag^+ + Cl^- \rightarrow AgCl$.

(C) $Ag^+ + Cl^- \rightarrow Ag + Cl$.

(D) $Ag + Cl \rightarrow Ag^+ + Cl^-$.

Your Answer _____

_____

147

Answers

Need to remember!

A–46

(B)

R — OH	alcohol
R — O — R^1	ether

$$\begin{matrix} & O \\ & \parallel \\ R & - C - H \end{matrix}$$ aldehyde

$$\begin{matrix} & O \\ & \parallel \\ R & - C - R^1 \end{matrix}$$ ketone

$$\begin{matrix} & O \\ & \parallel \\ R & - C - OH \end{matrix}$$ carboxylic acid

---

A–47

(A)   The equilibrium constant is given by the product of the concentrations of the products divided by the product of the reactant concentrations. Recall that the concentrations of solid products or reactants and water are omitted since they are assumed to be constant. This gives:

$$K = [Ag^+][Cl^-] \text{ for } AgCl \rightarrow Ag^+ + Cl^-$$

$$K = \frac{1}{[AG^+][Cl^-]} \text{ for } Ag^+ + Cl^- \rightarrow Ag$$

Atomic chlorine does not exist in nature, so the reactions proposed for it are irrelevant.

Questions

Q-48

Which of the following shifts the equilibrium of the following reaction to the right?

$$A_{(g)} + B_{(g)} + C_{(g)} \rightleftharpoons A_{(g)} + BC_{(g)} \quad (A)$$

(A) Addition of more A

(B) Removal of B

(C) Increasing the pressure

(D) Decreasing the temperature

Your Answer _____

_____

Q-49

Which of the following is a nonelectrolyte in water?

(A) Sodium nitrate   does not diss.

(B) Sulfuric acid

(C) Sodium bicarbonate

(D) Carbon tetrachloride

Your Answer _____

_____

Answers

A–48

(C) Addition of more *A* does not affect the equilibrium because *A* appears both as a reactant and a product. Removal of *B* causes the equilibrium to shift to the left. Increasing the pressure causes the system to move to the right in order to reduce the number of moles of gas present. Changes in temperature will not affect the equilibrium since there is no heat released to or absorbed from the environment during the reaction. The previous explanations are all based on Le Chatelier's Principle: a system when subjected to a stress will shift in a direction so as to minimize that stress.

A–49

(D) A nonelectrolyte is characterized by not dissociating in water solution. Of the choices given, only carbon tetrachloride satisfies this requirement.

Questions

Q–50

Which molecule among the following has the lowest molecular weight?

(A)

$$
\begin{array}{ccc}
H & H & H \\
| & | & | \\
H - C - C - C - H \\
| & | & | \\
H & H & H
\end{array}
$$

3 : C = 32
8 : H = 8
+
40

(B)

$$
\begin{array}{c}
H \\
| \\
H - C \equiv C - C - H \\
| \\
H
\end{array}
$$

3 : C = 32
4 : H = 4
+
36

(C)

$$
\begin{array}{cc}
H & H \\
\diagdown & | \\
C = C - C - H \\
\diagup & | \\
H & H
\end{array}
$$

3 : C = 32
5 : H = 5
+
37

(D) $H - C \equiv C - C \equiv C - H$

4 : C =
2 : H = 2

Your Answer _____

_____

Answers

A–50

(B)   It has only three carbon atoms and four hydrogen atoms.

   C: $3 \times 12 = 36$
   H: $4 \times 1 = 4$
   $36 + 4 = 40$, which is the molecular weight.

Questions

Q–51

What is the product of an alcohol after it under-goes a dehydration reaction?

(A) An aldehyde

(B) An alkane

(C) An alkene

(D) A carboxylic acid

$$\overset{O}{\underset{}{\overset{\|}{C}}}-H$$

Your Answer _____

_____

The Scottish scientist Sir Alexander Fleming discovered the antibiotic penicillin accidentally in 1928. He was culturing bacteria and he went on holiday. In his haste to go away he left the Petri dish lid ajar and when he returned a mold had killed the bacteria in the same dish. It took 10 years for scientists to extract the penicillin from the bacteria. (www.fashion-era.com)

Answers

A–51

(C) When an acid reacts with an alcohol, $-H_2O^+$ leaves the molecule, leaving behind an extra carbon-carbon double bond, resulting in an alkene.

Questions

Q–52

Which of the following structures represents 1, 1-dibromoethane?

(A)

$$Br-C-C-H$$

with Br and H above, H and H below the carbons

(B)

$$H-C-C-H$$

with Br and Br above, H and H below the carbons

(C) $CH_3 - CH_2 - Br - CH_2 - CH_3$

(D) $Br - C \equiv C - Br$

Your Answer _____

_____

Answers

(A) Dibromoethane is ethane, CH_3CH_3, with two hydrogen atoms replaced by bromine. The numbers "1,1" indicate that both bromine atoms are on the first carbon.

Thus

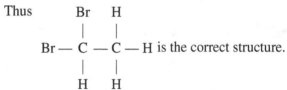 is the correct structure.

Questions

Questions 53 – 54 refer to the following:

$A_{(aq)} + 2B_{(aq)} \rightarrow C_{(aq)}$

The rate law for the reaction above is:

$$\text{rate} = K\,[B]^2$$

Q–53

What is the order of the reaction with respect to B?

(A) 0

(B) 1

(C) 2

(D) 3

Your Answer _____

✳A is not a factor

Q–54

What will happen to the rate of the reaction if the amount of A in the solution is doubled?

(A) The rate will double

(B) The rate will halve

(C) The rate will be four times bigger

(D) No effect

Your Answer _____

Answers

A–53

(C) The rate law includes the concentration of B raised to the second power, thus it is second order in B. The rate law includes no factor dependent on A and so it is zero order in A. The rate law is second order overall.

A–54

(D) Since A is not a factor in the rate law, changes in the concentration of A have no effect on the rate of reaction.

Questions

Q-55

Which of the following structures has the IUPAC name propyl butanoate?

(A) $CH_3CH_2CH_2OCH_2CH_2CH_2CH_3$

(B)
$$O$$
$$\|$$
$CH_3CH_2COCH_2CH_2CH_2CH_3$

(C)
$$O$$
$$\|$$
$CH_3CH_2CH_2CH_2COCH_2CH_2CH_3$

(D)
$$O$$
$$\|$$
$CH_3CH_2CH_2COCH_2CH_2CH_3$

but = 5
prop = 4

but
prop

Your Answer _____

_____

Q-56

Enzymes, which are organic catalysts, always at least partly consist of

(A) carbohydrates.

(B) lipids.

(C) nucleic acids.

(D) proteins.

Your Answer _____

_____

Answers

A–55

(D) The first word of the ester name is the name of the group attached to oxygen (propyl in our case). The second word is the name of the parent carboxylic acid with the suffix -*ic* replaced by -*ate* (butanoate in our case). Thus, we are looking for an ester with a propyl group attached to the oxygen of butanoic acid. This structure is

$$\overset{\displaystyle O}{\overset{\displaystyle \|}{}}$$

$$CH_3CH_2CH_2COCH_2CH_2CH_3$$

$CH_3CH_2CH_2OCH_2CH_2CH_2CH_3$ has the assigned name butyl propyl ether

$$\overset{\displaystyle O}{\overset{\displaystyle \|}{}}$$

$CH_3CH_2COCH_2CH_2CH_2CH_3$ has the assigned name butyl propanoate

$$\overset{\displaystyle O}{\overset{\displaystyle \|}{}}$$

$CH_3CH_2CH_2CH_2COCH_2CH_2CH_3$ has the assigned name propyl pentanoate

A–56

(D) Enzymes are proteins that act as catalysts for biochemical reactions.

Questions

Q–57

$Al(OH)_3$

Complete ionization of an aluminum hydroxide particle yields

(A) Al^+, OH^-.

(B) Al^+, $2OH^-$.

(C) Al^+, $3OH^-$.

(D) $2Al^+$, $3OH^-$.

Your Answer _____

_____

Q–58

An example of a molecule with a dipole is

(A) CH_4.

(B) H_2.

(C) H_2O.

(D) NaCl. (ionic)

Your Answer _____

_____

Answers

(C) Aluminum hydroxide's formula is $Al(OH)_3$. Thus, one aluminum ion and three hydroxyl ions are yielded by dissociation.

A–58

(C) A dipole is an electrical asymmetry in a molecule due to the unequal sharing of electron pairs between the spheres of bonding atoms. The two shared electron pairs of water spend more time in the command of oxygen's sphere than hydrogen's with its lower attracting power. Sodium chloride is not molecular but ionic. Methane (CH_4) and hydrogen gas share electron pairs equally and are thus nonpolar molecules. Sodium chloride is not molecular and thus does not have a dipole.

Questions

Question **59** refers to the valence electron dot formulas in the figure below. The letters merely identify the different atoms. They do not stand for actual known elements.

Valence Electron Dot Formulas

$$\overset{\cdot}{A} \qquad\qquad \overset{\cdot\cdot}{D}$$

$$\cdot \overset{\cdot}{\underset{\cdot}{X}} \cdot \qquad\qquad :\overset{\cdot\cdot}{\underset{\cdot}{Y}} \cdot$$

$$:\overset{\cdot\cdot}{\underset{\cdot\cdot}{Z}}:$$

Q–59

A possible compound by covalent bonding is

(A) AD_2.

(B) AX_3.

(C) XZ_4.

(D) YZ.

Your Answer _____

_____

Answers

(C)   Element X, with four electrons to offer, can satisfy four Z atoms, each in need of one electron for an outer, stable configuration of 8.

The American Chemical Society designated the 1940s research of Selman Waksman and his Rutgers University students into the actinomycete antibiotics a National Historic Chemical Landmark on May 24, 2005. They developed most notably the first effective treatment for tuberculosis, cholera, and typhoid fever. (www.acswebcontent.acs.org)

Questions

Q–60

In organic chemistry, the so-called aromatic behavior leads to

(A) addition reactions.

(B) substitution reactions.

(C) oxidation reactions.

(D) reduction reactions.

Your Answer _____

_____

Q–61

Which of the following interactions is primarily responsible for a protein's tertiary structure?

(A) Amide bonds

(B) Hydrogen bonds

(C) Sulfur-sulfur bonds

(D) Carbon-carbon bonds

Your Answer _____

_____

Answers

A–60

(B) The aromatic compounds are very stable, due to resonance, so substitution is most likely to happen.

A–61

(A) Disulfide bridges between cysteine residues on different parts of the amino acid sequence determine a protein's tertiary structure.

Questions

Q–62

The abbreviated electronic configuration of an element of atomic number 42 can be

(A) $[Kr]5s^14d^5$.

(B) $[Kr]5s^24d^4$.

(C) $[Kr]4d^6$.

(D) $[Kr]5s^25p^4$.

Your Answer _____

_____

Q–63

The animal cell membrane consists of a bilayer of

(A) proteins.

(B) carbohydrates.

(C) lipids.

(D) cellulose.

Your Answer _____

_____

Answers

A–62

(A) The abbreviated electronic configuration of an element of atomic number 42 is $[Kr]5s^1 4d^5$, where $[Kr]$ stands for the electronic arrangement of Krypton, element 36, indicating the filling of all sublevels through $4p^6$. The remaining 6 electrons go into $5s$ and $4d$ orbitals. The $5s^1 4d^5$ configuration is preferred over the $5s^2 4d^4$ configuration because of the stability of the half-filled $4d$ sublevel.

A–63

(C) The cell membrane consists of a semipermeable lipid bilayer, in which the nonpolar ends of the lipid molecules in each layer point inwards towards each other.

Questions

Q–64

The major role of carbon in biological systems is to

(A) provide complex branching structures.

(B) generate carbon dioxide.

(C) create energy.

(D) form cell walls.

Your Answer _____

_____

Medications are an integral part of space flight, used to treat space motion sickness, headache, sleeplessness, backache, and nasal congestion. With extended-duration space habitation, pharmacologic countermeasures will be used in part to respond to issues of nutritional status, musculoskeletal integrity, and immune response. (www.wylelabs.com)

Answers

A–64

(A)   Carbon has a unique capacity to form long chains, which result in its forming the basis of complex biomolecules. Waste carbon is emitted from the body in the form of carbon dioxide, but this is not the major role of carbon. Energy cannot be created, but it can be stored in the bonds of oxygen. Cell walls are only present in plant cells.

Questions

Q–65

What type of formula of ethane is depicted below?

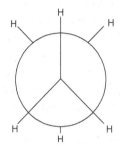

(A) Fisher projection formula

(B) Newman projection formula

(C) Lewis projection formula

(D) Kekulé projection formula

Your Answer _____

Q–66

According to Hund's rule, how many unpaired electrons does the ground state of iron have?

(A) 6

(B) 5

(C) 4

(D) 2

Your Answer _____

Answers

A–65

(B) Three-dimensional shapes of molecules are important to the chemist and biochemist. The Newman projection is a way of showing molecular conformations of alkanes. Conformations are the arrangements of atoms depending on the angle of rotation of one carbon with respect to another adjacent carbon. A Newman projection is obtained by looking at the molecule along the bond on which rotation occurs. The carbon in front is indicated by a point and at the back by a circle, the 3 remaining valences are placed 120° to each other (but remember that the bond angles about each of the carbon atoms are 109.5° and not 120° as the Newman projection formula might suggest).

A–66

(C) The ground state configuration of iron is $[Ar]4s^2 3d^6$. There are five d orbitals and with minimum pairing Fe has **4** unpaired electrons.

Questions

Q–67

Which of the following compounds have only nonpolar bonds?

(A) KO_2

(B) NaF

(C) HF

(D) I_2

Your Answer _____

_____

Q–68

Lithium (AW = 6.941) exists as two naturally occurring isotopes with relative atomic masses of 6.015 and 7.016. Find the percent abundances of the two isotopes.

(A) 23.1, 46.2

(B) 74.30, 25.70

(C) 90, 10

(D) 92.51, 7.49

Your Answer _____

_____

Answers

A–67

(D)   The polarity of a bond can be estimated by the difference in electronegativity (ΔEN) between the 2 atoms in the bond. The compounds in A to D are ionic (large ΔEN). ΔEN for I_2 is, of course, zero.

A–68

(D)   Let x = fraction of ^6_3Li and $1-x$ = fraction of ^7_3Li. $6.015x + 7.016 (1-x) = 6.941 \times x = .0749$ or 7.49%; $1-x = .9251$ or 92.51%.

Questions

Q–69

Which of the following molecules displays aromaticity?

(A) C_2H_4

(B) C_4H_6

(C) C_6H_6 → ben zene

(D) C_6H_{12}

answer
is wrong
in
book

Your Answer _____

_____

Q–70

Calculate the molecular weight of an unknown gas X if the ratio of its effusion rate to that of He is .378 (MW of He = 4.00).

(A) 9.47

(B) 42.3

(C) 10.6

(D) 28.0

Your Answer _____

_____

Answers

A-69

(A)   This is the chemical formula for benzene, which shares double bonds in a stable circular configuration.

A-70

(D)   Effusion rates of gases are related as $r_A / r_B = (MW_B / MW_A)^{1/2}$.

$$\frac{r_x}{r_{He}} = .378$$

$$.378 = \left(\frac{4.00}{r_{He}} \right)^{\frac{1}{2}}$$

$$MW_A = 28.0$$

Questions

Q-71

How many molecules are there in 22 g of CO_2?
The molecular weight of CO_2 is 44.

(A) 3

(B) 6.02×10^{23}

(C) 44

(D) 3.01×10^{23}

Your Answer _____

_____

$$(22g) \left(\frac{1 \text{mol}}{44g} \right) \left(\frac{6.02 \times 10^{23}}{1 \text{mol}} \right) =$$

Q-72

The sugar sucrose consists of

(A) glucose.

(B) fructose.

(C) a disaccharide of glucose and fructose.

(D) a disaccharide of glucose and aldose.

Your Answer _____

_____

Answers

(D)   The number of molecules in one mole is given by Avogadro's number which is: 1 mole of molecules contains 6.02×10^{23} molecules. Since the amount of CO_2 given is 22g it is first necessary to find the number of moles of CO_2 in 22g. This is calculated from:

$$moles = \frac{g}{MW} = \frac{22g}{44g/mol} = 0.5 \ moles \ of \ CO_2$$

It is now necessary to calculate the number of molecules in .5 moles of CO_2. This is obtained using Avogadro's number.

$$\frac{1 \ mole}{0.5 \ moles} = \frac{6.02g \times 10^{23} molecules}{x \ molecules}$$

$$x = 3.01 \times 10^{23} \ molecules$$

A-72

(C)   Sucrose is a disaccharide composed of two simple sugars, glucose and fructose.

Questions

Q-73

Which one of the following drawings represents the region of space an electron with a quantum number of $l = 1$ would be found?

(A) A

(B) B

(C) C

(D) D

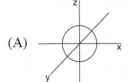

(A)

(B)

(C)

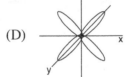

(D)

Your Answer _____

_____

Answers

(C)   The value of the azimuthal quantum number, l, may have values 0, l, 2 up to a maximum of $n - 1$, where n is the principal quantum number. The l value tells the subshell or orbital that the electron is in.

When $l = 0$ the electron is in an s orbital

  $l = 1$ the electron is in a p orbital

  $l = 2$ the electron is in a d orbital

The only p orbital that is shown is in diagram (C), which represents the p_z orbital since the lobes are going through the z axis.

  Answer   A   is an s orbital

      B   is the d_{x2-y2} orbital

      D   i the d_{xy} orbital

The correct answer is (C).

Questions

Q–74

In a protein, the peptide bonds that link together amino acids are

(A)   carbon-carbon bonds.

(B)   amide bonds.

(C))   phosphate bonds.

(D)   hydrogen bonds

Your Answer _____

_____

Q–75

Neutral atoms of F (fluorine) have the same number of electrons as

(A) N^+.

(B)) Ne^-.

(C) Na^-.

(D) Mg^{3+}.

Your Answer _____

_____

Answers

A-74

(B) The peptide bonds in a protein are amide bonds, where a nitrogen in an amino acid is bonded to a carbon bond on the opposite side of another amino acid. Hydrogen bonds are found between opposite base pairs in DNA, and phosphate bonds are also found in DNA.

A-75

(D) Neutral fluorine atoms have 9 electrons as determined by their atomic number. Magnesium atoms have 12 electrons so Mg^{3+} has 9 electrons. Nitrogen has 7 electrons so N^+ has 6 electrons (the same as carbon). Neon has 10 electrons so Ne^- has 11 electrons (the same as sodium). Sodium has 11 electrons so Na^- has 12 electrons (the same as magnesium).

Questions

Q-76

The molecular weight of a gas is 16. At STP, 4.48 liters of this gas weighs

(A) 2.3g.

(B) 2.7g.

(C) 3.2g.

(D) 4.1g.

Your Answer _____

_____

$$\frac{16g}{1 \, mol}$$

Q-77

How many moles of electrons are required to reduce 103.6g of lead from Pb^{2+} to the metal?

(A) 0.5 mole

(B) 1 mole

(C) 2 moles

(D) 4 moles

Your Answer _____

_____

Answers

A–76

(C)   A molecular weight of 16g tells us that a volume of 22.4 liters (molar volume) of that gas weighs 16g. To determine the weight of a 4.48 L sample we multiply

$$4.48L \times \frac{16g}{22.4L} = 3.2g$$

A–77

(B)   The atomic weight of lead is 207.2g/mole from the periodic table. The number of moles present in 103.6g of lead is given by

$$103.6g \times \frac{1\ mole}{207.2g} = 0.5\ mole$$

Since lead is in the +2 oxidation state, two moles of electrons are required for every mole of lead to reduce it to the metals. However, only one mole of electrons is required to reduce 0.5 mole of Pb^{2+} to Pb^0.

Questions

Q–78

What is the molecular weight of $HClO_4$?

(A)   52.5

(B)   73.5

(C)   96.5

(D)   100.5

$H = 1$

$Cl = 35$

$O = 16(4)$

Your Answer _____

Q–79

The systematic (IUPAC) name of this structure is

```
     H   H   H   OH   H   H
     |   |   |   |    |   |
H — C — C — C — C  — C — C — H
     |   |   |   |    |   |
     H   H   H   H    H   H
```

(A)   hexanol.

(B)   3-hydroxyhexane.

(C)   3-hexanol.

(D)   4-hexanol.

Your Answer _____

Answers

A-78

(D)   The molecular weight of a compound is the sum of its constituents' atomic weights. Elements or groups followed by a subscript have their atomic weight multiplied by that subscript. Thus, the molecular weight of perchloric acid ($HClO_4$) is atomic weight of H + atomic weight of Cl + 4 × atomic weight of O
or $l + 35.5 + 4(16) = 100.5$

A-79

(C)   Alcohols are named by replacing the -*e* of the corresponding hydrocarbon name by the suffix -*ol*. The position of the hydroxy substituent is numbered from the shorter end of the chain. Thus, the structure is named 3-hexanol. It is a hexanol because the parent hydrocarbon has six carbons and the prefix 3- (not 4-) is used to indicate the location of the hydroxy group on the third carbon.

Questions

Q–80

Which of the elements in Group IA of the periodic table has the greatest metallic character?

(A) Li

(B) Na

(C) K

(D) Fr

Your Answer _____

_____

Q–81

Which of the following serves as a catalyst in the reaction

$$CH_2 = CH_2 + H_2 + Pt \rightarrow CH_3CH_3 + Pt$$

(A) C

(B) $CH_2 = CH_2$

(C) H_2

(D) Pt

Your Answer _____

_____

Answers

A–80

(D)   The metals are found on the left side of the periodic table, with metallic character increasing as one goes down a group. All the choices given are in Group IA, so the one farthest down in the group has the greatest metallic character. This is francium (Fr).

A–81

(D)   One characteristic of a catalyst is that it remains unchanged by the reaction process. It may now be seen that the platinum, Pt, is the catalyst for this reaction.

Questions

Q–82

The expected electron configuration of propanal is:

(A)
$$
\begin{array}{ccc}
\text{H} & \text{H} & \text{H} \\
\text{H} : \overset{..}{\underset{..}{\text{C}}} : \overset{..}{\underset{..}{\text{C}}} : \overset{..}{\text{C}} : \overset{..}{\underset{..}{\text{O}}} : \\
\text{H} & \text{H}
\end{array}
$$

(B)
$$
\begin{array}{ccc}
\text{H} & \text{H} & \text{H} \\
\text{H} : \overset{..}{\text{C}} : : \text{C} : \overset{..}{\text{C}} : \overset{..}{\underset{..}{\text{O}}} : \\
 & \text{H}
\end{array}
$$

(C)
$$
\begin{array}{cc}
\text{H} & \text{H} \\
\text{H} : \overset{..}{\text{C}} : : \text{C} : : \overset{..}{\text{C}} : \text{O}
\end{array}
$$

(D)
$$
\begin{array}{ccc}
\text{H} & \text{H} & \text{H} \\
\text{H} : \overset{..}{\underset{..}{\text{C}}} : \overset{..}{\text{C}} : \overset{..}{\text{C}} : : \overset{..}{\underset{..}{\text{O}}} : \\
\text{H} & \text{H}
\end{array}
$$

Your Answer _____

_____

The FDA Approved Animal Drug Products (Green Book), is published by the Drug Information Laboratory; paper copies are available by subscription. (www.fda.gov)

Answers

(D)   From the name propanal, we find that we must describe an aldehyde (from the -al suffix) composed of a 3-carbon skeleton (from the prop- prefix) with no multiple bonds (from the -ane root). Remembering that an aldehyde is characterized by the functional group

$$\begin{array}{c} O \\ \| \\ -C-H \end{array}$$

we obtain

$$\begin{array}{c} O \\ \| \\ CH_3-CH_2-C-H \end{array}$$

as a result. This is equivalent to the electron configuration in (D), since each bond (1) represents two electrons.

Questions

Q–83

The attractive force between the protons of one molecule and the electrons of another molecule is strongest

(A) in the solid phase.

(B) in the liquid phase.

(C) in the gas phase.

(D) during sublimation.

Your Answer _____

_____

Q–84

The oxidation state of manganese in $\overset{+1}{K}\overset{}{Mn}\overset{-2}{O}_4$ is

(A) +1.

(B) +2.

-8

(C) +3.

(D) +7.

Your Answer _____

_____

Answers

A–83

(A) The attractive force between the protons of one atom and the electrons of another is inversely proportional to the distance between the atoms, i.e., $(F \propto 1/d)$ where F = force and d = distance between two atoms. This shows that the attraction is strongest at small distances (as in solids) and weakest at large distances (as in gases).

A–84

(D) The oxidation states of the atoms of a neutral compound must add up to equal zero. For $KMnO_4$, the oxidation state of K must be $+1$ since it is in Group IA and the oxidation state of O must be -2 since it is in Group VIA. Thus we have:

$$1 + Mn + 4(-2) = 0 \text{ and } Mn = +7$$

Questions

Q-85

An increase in pressure will change the equilibrium constant by

(A) shifting to the side where a smaller volume results.

(B) shifting to the side where a larger volume results.

(C) favoring the exothermic reaction.

(D) None of the above.

Your Answer _____

_____

Q-86

The most active metal of the alkali metals is

(A) Li.

(B) Mg.

(C) K.

(D) Cs.

Your Answer _____

_____

Answers

A–85

(D) The equilibrium constant is independent of pressure and volume but dependent on temperature.

A–86

(D) Activity increases as one moves down a group of the periodic table since the outermost electrons are further away from the nucleus and not held as tightly as those of the smaller atoms. Also, metallic character is greatest at the far left of the periodic table.

Questions

Q–87

A gas has a volume of 10 liters at 50°C and 200mm Hg pressure. What correction factor is needed to give a volume at STP?

(A) $\frac{0}{50} \times \frac{200}{760}$

(B) $\frac{0}{50} \times \frac{760}{200}$

(C) $\frac{273}{323} \times \frac{200}{760}$

(D) $\frac{273}{323} \times \frac{760}{200}$

Your Answer _____

_____

$$\begin{array}{r} \cancel{116}^{\,0\,10} \\ -48 \\ \hline 68 \end{array}$$

$HNO_3 + LiOH \rightarrow$
$\qquad\qquad LiNO_3 + H_2O$

Q–88

How much reactant remains if 92g of HNO_3 is reacted with 24g of LiOH assuming the reaction to be complete?

(A) 46g of HNO_3

(B) 29g of HNO_3

(C) 12g of HNO_3

(D) 2g of LiOH

see answer 2

$$\begin{array}{r} ^{e}\!\!\cancel{9}12 \\ -24 \\ \hline 68 \end{array}$$

$$\begin{array}{r} 92 \\ +24 \\ \hline 116 \end{array}$$

$$\begin{array}{r} 24 \\ +24 \\ \hline 48 \end{array}$$

Your Answer _____

_____

195

Answers

A–87

(C)   This problem is solved by applying the combined as law:

$$\frac{P_1 V_1}{T_1} = \frac{P_2 V_2}{T_2}$$

Rearranging gives:

$$V_2 = V_1 \times \frac{T_2}{T_1} \times \frac{P_1}{P_2}$$

Substituting given values:

$$V_2 = 10 \times \frac{273}{323} \times \frac{200}{760}$$

This gives the correction factor:

$$\frac{273}{323} \times \frac{200}{760}$$

A–88

(B)   The molecular weight of HNO_3 is 63 grams/mole and that of $LiOH$ is 24 grams/mole. HNO_3 and $LiOH$ react in a 1:1 ratio by mole as seen by

$$HNO_3 + LiOH \rightarrow H_2O + LiNO_3$$

There is an excess of HNO_3, since only one mole of it can react with the one mole of $LiOH$ available. Thus, there is an excess of 92 – 63 or 29 grams of nitric acid.

Questions

Q–89

What is the density of a diatomic gas whose gram-molecular weight is 80g?

(A) 1.9g/liter

(B) 2.8g/liter

(C) 3.6g/liter

(D) 4.3g/liter

$$\frac{80 g/mol}{22.4 L/mol} \qquad D = \frac{m}{V}$$

Your Answer _____

_____

Q–90

In the compound $HClO_2$, the chlorine atom has an oxidation number of

(A) –3.

(B) +1.

(C) +3.

(D) +5.

$$H^+ Cl \; O_2^{-2}$$

$$+1 \qquad -4$$

Your Answer _____

_____

Answers

A–89

(C)   Recalling that density equals

$$\rho = \frac{m}{v}$$

gives $\rho = \dfrac{80g/mole}{22.4l/mole} = 3.6 g/liter$

A–90

(C)   The oxidation number of hydrogen in this compound is +1, and the oxidation number of oxygen is –2. To add up to a neutral compound, the oxidation number of chlorine must therefore be calculated as $0 = 1 + 2(-2) + x$;
$x = +3$.

Questions

Q–91

Which statement is true for a liquid/gas mixture in equilibrium?

(A) The equilibrium constant is dependent on temperature.

(B) The amount of the gas present at equilibrium is independent of pressure.

(C) All interchange between the liquid and gas phases has ceased.

(D) All of the above.

Your Answer _____

Q–92

Calculate the concentration of HI present in an equilibrium mixture produced by the reaction

$$H_{2(g)} + I_{2(g)} \rightleftharpoons 2HI_{(g)}$$ if $K_e = 3.3 \times 10^{-1}$

and the concentrations of H_2 and I_2 are 0.1M and 0.3M, respectively, at equilibrium.

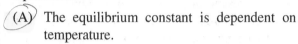

0.1   0.3

(A) 0.01M

(B) 0.03M

(C) 0.05M

(D) 0.1M

$$K_e = \frac{[HI]^2}{[H_2][I_2]}$$

$$(33)(0.1)(0.3) = [HI]^2$$

$$0.99 = [HI]^2$$

$$0.03$$

work backwards

Your Answer _____

199

Answers

A-91

(A) The equilibrium constant is dependent only on temperature but the amount of each substance present at equilibrium is dependent on pressure, volume, and temperature. There is still an interchange between the phases, but the same number of molecules leave and enter both phases so the equilibrium concentrations and equilibrium constant are the same for a given pressure, volume, and temperature.

A-92

(D) The equilibrium constant expression for the reaction is:

$$K_e = \frac{[HI]^2}{[H_2][I_2]}$$

Substituting given values, we obtain:

$$3.3 \times 10^{-1} = \frac{[HI]^2}{(0.1)(0.3)}$$

Rearranging:

$[HI]^2 = (3.3 \times 10^{-1})(0.1)(0.3) = 9.9 \times 10^{-3}$

and $[HI] = 0.1\ M$

Questions

Q–93

The production of alkanes from alkenes is accomplished by

(A) burning in the presence of water.

(B) distillation.

(C) methylation.

(D) catalytic hydrogenation.

Your Answer _____

_____

Q–94

sp^2 hybridization will be found for carbon in

(A) CH_4. ← tetrahedral

(B) C_2H_4. ← $H-C=C-H$ (with H above and below)

(C) C_2H_2.

(D) CH_3OH.

Your Answer _____

_____

Answers

(D) Hydrogenation using a metal catalyst is a common method of producing alkanes from alkenes.

$$C_2H_4 + H_2 \xrightarrow{Pt} C_2H_6$$

Good trick!

A–94

(B) A simple method for determining hybridization in carbon compounds is by determining how many atoms are attached to the carbon atom. If two atoms are attached, the hybridization is sp, if three, sp^2, and if four, sp^3. Thus,

$H — C \equiv C — H$ has sp hybridization

$$
\begin{array}{c}
H \qquad\qquad H \\
\diagdown \qquad\quad \diagup \\
C = C \\
\diagup \qquad\quad \diagdown \\
H \qquad\qquad H
\end{array}
$$
has sp^2 hybridization

$$
\begin{array}{c}
H \quad H \\
| \quad\; | \\
H — C — C — H \\
| \quad\; | \\
H \quad H
\end{array}
$$
has sp^3 hybridization

Questions

Q–95

How many grams of Cu could be produced from $CuSO_4$ by 0.5 faradays of charge?

(A) 15.9

(B) 31.75

(C) 63.5

(D) 127.0

Your Answer _____

_____

$CO_2 + H_2O = H_2CO_3$

Q–96

Reacting $CO_2(g)$ with water results in the production of

(A)   methane and oxygen.

(B)   carbonous acid.

(C)   carbonic acid. ←

(D)   carbon and oxygen.

Your Answer _____

_____

Answers

A-95

(A)   A faraday is the amount of electricity that allows the reaction of one mole of electrons. Each Cu^{2+} ion requires two electrons to be reduced to elemental copper.

$$0.5F \times \frac{\text{one mole } Cu^{2+} \text{ reduced to } Cu}{2F}$$

$= 0.25$ mole of Cu^{2+} reduced to Cu

Since the atomic weight of copper is 63.5g/mole, we have

$$0.25 \text{ mole} \times \frac{63.5g}{1 \text{ mole}} = 15.9g \text{ of Cu.}$$

A-96

(C) CO_2 is an acid anhydride since an acid is produced upon reaction with water

$$CO_{2(g)} + H_2O \rightarrow H_2CO_3 \text{ (carbonic acid)}$$

Questions

Q–97

What is K_b for a $0.1M$ solution of NH_4OH if $[OH^-]$ $= 1.3 \times 10^{-3}$?

(A) 7.6×10^{-1}

(B) 1.1×10^{-2}

(C) 4.2×10^{-3}

(D) 1.7×10^{-5}

Your Answer _____

_____

Q–98

How many grams of HNO_3 are required to produce a one liter aqueous solution of pH 2?

(A) 0.063

(B) 0.63

(C) 6.3

(D) 1.26

Your Answer _____

_____

Answers

A–97

(D) K_b, the base dissociation constant, is defined as

$$K_b = \frac{[X^+][OH^-]}{[XOH]}$$

Since $[OH^-] = 1.3 \times 10^{-3}$ we know that $= 1.3 \times 10^{-3}$ and that the original concentration of NH_4OH is 0.1M. Substituting values we obtain

$$K_b = \frac{(1.3\times 10^{-3})(1.3\times 10^{-3})}{(0.1 - 1.3\times 10^{-3})} = \frac{1.69\times 10^{-6}}{0.0987}$$

$K_b = 1.7 \times 10^{-5}$

A–98

(B) The pH of a solution is defined as
$pH = -\log[H^+]$
Solving for $[H^+]$, we obtain
$[H^+] = 10^{-pH} = 10^{-2}$
Nitric acid is assumed to dissociate completely in solution since it is a strong acid. In addition, nitric acid has only one proton so the concentration of hydronium ions is equal to the initial concentration of HNO_3. We are working with one liter of solution so the concentration is identical to the number of moles by

$$M = \frac{number\ of\ moles\ of\ solute}{liters\ of\ solution}$$

Thus, we require 10^{-2} mole of HNO_3. Converting to grams:

$$10.2\ \text{mole of}\ HNO_3 \times \frac{63g\ of\ HNO_3}{1\ mole\ of\ HNO_3} = 0.63g$$

of HNO_3

Questions

Q-99

A one liter solution of 2*M* NaOH can be prepared with

(A) 20g of NaOH.

(B) 40g of NaOH.

(C) 60g of NaOH.

(D) 80g of NaOH.

handwritten: $\dfrac{2 \, mol}{1 \, L}$

handwritten margin:
$$23$$
$$16$$
$$+ \ 1$$
$$\overline{40g}$$

Your Answer _____

_____

handwritten:
$$\left(\frac{2mol}{1L}\right)\left(\frac{40g}{1mol}\right) = \ 80g$$

Q-100

What is/are the product gas/gases if NH$_4$Cl and Ca(OH)$_2$ are used as reactants?

(A) N$_2$

(B) NH$_3$

(C) H$_2$O

(D) NH$_3$ + H$_2$O

handwritten: $NH_4 Cl + Ca(OH)_2 \rightarrow$

handwritten margin: do NOT 2nd guess! 2

Your Answer _____

_____

Answers

A–99

(D)   Molarity is defined as the number of moles of solute divided by the number of liters of solution. Thus,

$$M = \frac{moles\ of\ solute}{liters\ of\ solution}$$

Rearranging,

moles of solute = (M) (liters of solution)

$$= (2)\,(1)$$
$$= 2$$

Converting to grams:

$$2\,moles\ of\ NaOH \times \frac{40g\ of\ NaOH}{1\ mole\ of\ NaOH} = 80g\ of\ NaOH$$

A–100

(D)   The reaction is

$$2NH_4Cl_{(s)} + Ca(OH)_{2(s)} \rightarrow CaCl_2 + 2H_2O_{(g)} + 2NH_{3(g)}$$

Questions

Q–101

Which of the following is incorrect?

(A) 1 liter = 1,000 cm³

(B) 1 meter = 100 cm

(C) 1 milliliter = 1 cm³

(D) 1 liter = 1 meter³

Your Answer _____

Book is wrong!

Q–102

When sulfur ionizes, it most often carries a charge of

(A) –1.

(B) –2. ← correct!

(C) +2.

(D) +5.

Your Answer _____

Answers

A–101

(D) The correct expression would be

$$1 \text{ liter} = 1,000 \text{ } cm^3 \times \left(\frac{1 m}{100 \text{ } cm} \right)^3$$

$$1 \text{ liter} = 1,000 \text{ } cm^3 \times \frac{1 m^3}{1 \times 10^6 \text{ } cm^3}$$

$$1 \text{ liter} = 1 \times 10^{-3} \text{ } m^3$$

A–102

(A) The electronic configuration of sulfur is $1s^2$ $2s^2 2p^6 3s^2 3p^4$ as given by the periodic table. Thus, it needs two electrons to fill its $3p$ energy level to give it the same electronic configuration as Ar, and therefore it tends to ionize with a 2– charge.

Questions

Q–103

The oxidizing agent in the reaction

$Pb + HgSO_4 \rightarrow PbSO_4 + Hg$ is

(A) Pb.

(B) $PbSO_4$.

(C) Hg^{+2}.

(D) Hg^0.

Your Answer _____

_____

LEO

Q–104

The relation between the absolute temperature and volume of a gas at constant pressure is given by

(A) Boyle's Law.

(B) Charles's Law.

(C) the combined gas law.

(D) the ideal gas law.

Your Answer _____

_____

Answers

A–103

(C)   The oxidizing agent in the reaction is the reagent that gains electron oxidizing another element or compound in a redox reaction.

$$Pb^0 + Hg^{+2}SO_4^{-2} \rightarrow Pb^{+2}SO_4^{-2} + Hg^0$$

We see that Hg^{+2} served as an oxidizing agent by oxidizing Pb, while also becoming reduced.

A–104

(B)   Charles's Law states that the volume of a gas varies directly with the absolute temperature at constant pressure.

Questions

Q–105

Which of the following would produce a highly conductive aqueous solution.

(A) Cyclohexane

(B) Hydrochloric acid

(C) Benzene

(D) Acetic acid

Your Answer _____

_____

Book is wrong!

Q–106

Which of the following is the strongest acid?

(A) $HClO$

(B) $HClO_2$

(C) $HClO_3$

(D) $HClO_4$ *right!*

Your Answer _____

_____

Answers

A–105

(B) The conductivity of a solution is directly related to the number of ions in solution. Hydrochloric acid, being a strong acid, dissociates completely while acetic acid, a weak acid, is only slightly dissociated. Cyclohexane and benzene may be said to be undissociated in solution.

A–106

(C) $HClO_4$, perchloric acid, is the strongest acid because it has the most oxygen atoms, which are electronegative and draw electrons to themselves, making it easiest for H^+ to ionize.

Questions

Q–107

All of the following are spontaneous reactions EXCEPT

$$Co^{+2} + 2e^- \rightarrow Co \qquad E° = -0.28V$$
$$Sn^{+2} + 2e^- \rightarrow Sn \qquad E° = -0.14V$$
$$Zn^{+2} + 2e^- \rightarrow Zn \qquad E° = -0.76V$$
$$Fe^{+2} + 2e^- \rightarrow Fe \qquad E° = -0.44V$$
$$Mg^{+2} + 2e^- \rightarrow Mg \qquad E° = -2.37V$$
$$F_2 + 2e^- \rightarrow 2F^- \qquad E° = +2.87V$$
$$Cn^{+2} + 2e^- \rightarrow Mn \qquad E° = -1.18V$$
$$2(Li^{+1} + e^- \rightarrow Li) \qquad E° = -3.00V$$
$$2\,(Ag^{+1} + e^- \rightarrow Ag) \qquad E° = +0.80V$$

(A) $Co^{2+} + Zn \rightarrow Zn^{2+} + Co$

(B) $Mg^{2+} + Mn \rightarrow Mn^{2+} + Mg$

(C) $2Ag^+ + H_2 \rightarrow 2H^+ + 2Ag$

(D) $Sn^{2+} + Fe \rightarrow Fe^{2+} + Sn$

Your Answer _____

Answers

A–107

(B) Using the standard electrode potentials and recalling that a positive value indicates that the reaction is spontaneous while a negative value shows that the reverse reaction is spontaneous:

$Co^{2+} + 2e^- \rightarrow Co$	$E° = -0.28V$
$Zn \rightarrow Zn^{2+} + 2e^-$	$E° = +0.76V$
$Co^{2+} + Zn \rightarrow Zn^{2+} + Co$	$E° = +0.48V$
$Mg^{2+} + 2e^- \rightarrow Mg$	$E° = -2.37V$
$Mn \rightarrow Mn^{2+} + 2e^-$	$E° = +1.18V$
$Mg^{2+} + Mn \rightarrow Mn^{2+} + Mg$	$E° = -1.19V$
$2(Ag^+ + e^- \rightarrow Ag)$	$E° = +0.80V$
$H_2 \rightarrow 2H^+ + 2e^-$	$E° = 0.00V$
$2Ag^+ + H_2 \rightarrow 2H^+ + 2Ag$	$E° = +0.80V$
$Sn^{2+} + 2e^- \rightarrow Sn$	$E° = -0.14V$
$Fe \rightarrow Fe^{2+} + 2e^-$	$E° = +0.44V$
$Sn^{2+} + Fe \rightarrow Fe^{2+} + Sn$	$E° = +0.30V$
$F_2 + 2e^- \rightarrow 2F^-$	$E° = +2.87V$
$2(Li \rightarrow Li^+ + e^-)$	$E° = +3.00V$
$F_2 + 2Li \rightarrow 2Li^+ + 2F^-$	$E° = +5.87V$

Questions

Q–108

What is X in the reaction $X + {}_1^1H \rightarrow {}_6^{12}C + {}_2^4He$?

(A) ${}_7^{15}O$

(B) ${}_7^{15}N$

(C) ${}_9^{17}F$

(D) ${}_9^{17}O$

15   16

7   8

Your Answer _____

_____

Q–109

An example of an acid salt is

(A) NaCl.

(B) Na_2SO_4.

(C) $NaHCO_3$.

(D) $Mg(HSO_4)_2$.

Your Answer _____

_____

Answers

A–108

(B) The total composition of the products must equal that of the reactants. Summing the number of protons and the atomic masses of the products we have $6 + 2 = 8$ protons and an atomic mass of $12 + 4 = 16$. Subtracting $_1^1H$, we have $_7^{15}X$. The atomic number 7 corresponds to nitrogen, so we have $_7^{15}N$.

A–109

(D) An acid salt yields an acidic solution upon hydrolysis.

$$NaCl + H_2O \rightarrow HCl + NaOH$$

The solution produced by $NaCl$ is neutral since HCl is a strong acid and $NaOH$ is a strong base.

$$Na_2SO_4 + 2H_2O \rightarrow H_2SO_4 + 2NaOH$$

This is also a neutral solution since H_2SO_4 is a strong acid.

$$NaHCO_3 + H_2O \rightarrow H_2CO_3 + NaOH$$

A basic solution is produced by hydrolysis of $NaHCO_3$ since H_2CO_3 is a weak acid. Therefore $NaHCO_3$ is a basic salt.

$$Mg(HSO_4)_2 + 2H_2O \rightarrow H_2SO_4 + Mg(OH)_2$$

$Mg(HSO_4)_2$ is an acid salt since hydrolysis produces a strong acid and a weak base.

Questions

Q-110

How many moles of ions are present in a saturated one liter solution of $BaSO_4$ ($K_{sp} = 1.1 \times 10^{-10}$)?

(A) 1×10^{-10}

(B) 2×10^{-10}

(C) 4×10^{-10}

(D) 2×10^{-5}

Your Answer _____

_____

A barrier isolator is new technology for hospital pharmacy departments. The barrier isolator is used when preparing intravenous medications to ensure a completely sterile environment. (www.uspharmd.com)

Answers

A–110

(D) The solubility product of $BaSO_4$ is given by

$$K_{sp} = [Ba^{2+}] [SO_4^{2-}] = 1.1 \times 10^{-10}$$

where $[Ba^{2+}]$ and $[SO_4^{2-}]$ are the concentrations of Ba^{2+} and SO_4^{2-} in solution, respectively. It is necessary, stoichiometrically, that $[Ba^{2+}] = [SO_4^{2-}]$ so if we let $x = [Ba^{2+}] = [SO_4^{2-}]$, we have

$$K_{sp} = x^2 = 1.1 \times 10^{-10}$$

and $x = \sqrt{1.1 \times 10^{-10}} = 1 \times 10^{-5}$

The total number of ions present in a saturated one liter solution is given by the sum of the concentrations of the individual species present. Note that this is true only if the solution is of one liter volume. Since the molarity is the number of moles per liter of total solution, then for one liter of total solution, the total number of ions is given by:

$$[Ba^{2+}] + [SO_4^{2-}] = 1 \times 10^{-5} + 1 \times 10^{-5} = 2 \times 10^{-5}$$

Questions

Q–111

What is the boiling point of an aqueous solution containing 117g of NaCl in 1,000g of H_2O?

$Kb (H_2O) = 0.52°$ C-kg/mol

(A) 98.96°C

(B) 99.48°C

(C) 100.52°C

(D) 102.08°C

Your Answer _____

117

0.117

$NaCl + H_2O \rightarrow$

Q–112

The sum of the coefficients of the reaction

_4_ C_6H_6 + ___O_2 → _24_CO_2 + _12_H_2O

when it is balanced is

12 + 3 = 15 : o

6 : C

6 : H

(A) 7.

(B) 14.

(C) 28.

(D) 35.

see given balanced

Your Answer _____

Answers

A-111

(D) Converting to moles:

$$117g \text{ of } NaCl \times \frac{1 \text{ mole of } NaCl}{58.5 \text{ g of } NaCl} = 2 \text{ moles of } NaCl$$

The molality of a solution is defined as the number of moles of dissolved solute per 1,000g of solvent. Therefore the molality of the solution is $2m$ in $NaCl$. However, since $NaCl$ dissociates completely to Na^+ and Cl^-, the molality of the solution is $4m$ in particles. It has been found that a $1m$ aqueous solution freezes at $-1.86°C$ and boils at $100.52°C$, a change of $-1.86°C$ and $+0.52°C$, respectively. Thus, the boiling point increase for a $4m$ solution (since boiling point elevation is a colligative property) is

$$4m \times \frac{0.52°C}{1m} = 2.08°C$$

Therefore, the boiling point of the solution is
$$100°C + 2.08°C = 102.08°C$$

A-112

(D) The balanced reaction is

$$C_6H_6 + \frac{15}{2}O_2 \rightarrow 6CO_2 + 3H_2O$$

Since the carbon in CO_2 can only be obtained from benzene, which has 6 carbons, we know that the coefficient of CO_2 will be 6. In a similar fashion, the coefficient of H_2O will be 3 since benzene has 6 hydrogens. There are 12 oxygens in $6CO_2$ and 3 oxygens in $3H_2O$ so the coefficient of O_2 is $^{15}/_2$. Multiplying by 2 to remove the fraction, we obtain
$$2C_6H_6 + 15O_2 \rightarrow 12CO_2 + 6H_2O$$

Questions

Q–113

How many orbitals can one find in a p subshell?

(A) 2

(B) 3

(C) 6

(D) 7

Your Answer _____

_____

s^2

p^6

d^{10}

f^{16}

Q–114

Which of the following is a chemical property?

(A) Melting point

(B) Density

(C) Viscosity

(D) Burning

Your Answer _____

_____

Answers

Need to Know!

A–113

(B)   The number of orbitals in a subshell is described by the quantum number m_l in the following manner:

subshell	l	$m_l = 2l + 1$
s	0	1
p	1	3
d	2	5
f	3	7

A–114

(D)   A chemical property is one that refers to the way in which a substance is able to change into other substances—its reactivity. Burning is the process of uncontrolled oxidation. Choices A through C are physical properties—those that do not involve a change in the chemical identity of the substance.

Questions

Q–115

What is the pOH of a solution with $[H^+] = 1 \times 10^{-3}$?

(A) −3

(B) 1

(C) 3

(D) 11

$pH = -\log(1 \times 10^{-3})$

$pH = 3$

$pOH = 11$

Your Answer _____

$$m_1 V_1 = m_2 V_2$$

Q–116

A student titrates 100 ml of acid with $5M$ NaOH. Phenolphthalein indicator changes color after 50 ml of NaOH have been added. What is the molarity of the monoprotic acid?

(A) 0.1M

(B) 1M

(C) 1.5M

(D) 2.5M

$\left(\dfrac{5 \, mol}{L}\right)(0.05L)$

K

H

D

4

D

C

m

50.

.05 L

Your Answer _____

Answers

A–115

(D)   Using the definition of pH, we find that
$$pH = -\log[H^+] = 3$$
Since $pH + pOH = 14$, we have $pOH = 11$.

A–116

(D)   Since $M_1 V_1 = M_2 V_2$, we have

$$M_2 = \frac{M_1 V_1}{V_2} = \frac{(5)(50)}{100} = 2.5$$

Questions

Q–117

The normal electronic configuration of chlorine gas is

(A) Cl̈ : Cl̈

(B) : C̈l : C̈l : → *complete octet* C̈l ∘

(C) Cl̈ : : Cl̈

(D) : Cl : : Cl :

Your Answer _____

_____

Na Cl

Q–118

Molecules of sodium chloride

(A) display ionic bonding.

(B) display polar covalent bonding.

(C) are polar.

(D) do not exist.

Your Answer _____

_____

Answers

A–117

(B) The most stable electronic configuration of a molecule is that in which each atom has a complete octet of electrons surrounding it. Chlorine, being in Group VIIA has seven electrons in its valence shell. Therefore, Cl_2 has 14 electrons. This leads to the structure

$$:\overset{..}{\underset{..}{Cl}} : \overset{..}{\underset{..}{Cl}}:$$

A–118

(D) Molecules of sodium chloride do not exist individually. Rather sodium and chloride ions occupy points in a crystal lattice structure.

Questions

Q–119

An element, A, forms a sulfide with the formula AS. Which of the following formulas would represent that sulfide?

(A) ABr

(B) AO_2

(C) AH_2

(D) A_2O_3

Your Answer _____

$Fe = 56$
$O = 16$

Q–120

Which is the empirical formula of a compound consisting of 70% iron and 30% oxygen by mass?

(A) FeO

(B) FeO_2

(C) Fe_2O

(D) Fe_2O_3

Your Answer _____

229

Answers

A–119

(C) Sulfur has a common oxidation state of –2. Therefore, A must have an oxidation state of +2. The bromide of A would be ABr_2 since bromine has an oxidation state of –1. The oxide of A would have the same formula as the sulfide. The hydrogens in a hydride have an oxidation state of –1 so the hydride of A would have the formula AH_2.

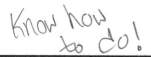

Know how to do!

A–120

(D) A 100g sample of this compound would contain 70g of iron and 30g of oxygen. Converting these weights to moles

$$70\text{g of } Fe \times \frac{1 \text{ mole of } Fe}{56 \text{ g of } O} = 1.25 \text{ moles of } Fe$$

$$30\text{g of } O \times \frac{1 \text{ mole of } O}{16 \text{ g of } O} = 1.9 \text{ moles of } O$$

This gives an empirical formula of $Fe_{1.25} O_{1.9}$. We convert to whole numbers by dividing each subscript by the smallest subscript:

$$Fe_{\frac{1.25}{1.25}} O_{\frac{1.9}{1.25}} = FeO_{1.52}$$

Multiplying each subscript by 2 to obtain integer values, we obtain Fe_2O_3.

Questions

Q–121

What is the IUPAC name for the structure below?

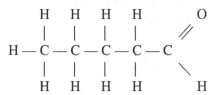

(A) Butanal

(B) Pentanal

(C) Butanol

(D) Pentanol

Your Answer _____

_____

Q–122

What is the electronic configuration of sulfur?

(A) $1s^2\ 2s^2\ 2p^8\ 3s^2\ 3p^2$

(B) $1s^2\ 2s^2\ 2p^6\ 3s^2\ 3p^4$

(C) $1s^2\ 2s^2\ 3s^2\ 2p^8\ 3p^2$

(D) $1s^2\ 2s^2\ 2p^8\ 3s^2\ 3p^8$

Your Answer _____

_____

Answers

A–121

(B)   The carbon skeleton of this molecule contains five carbons so we name it with the prefix *pentan-*. The molecule contains the functional group of an aldehyde, which gives us the suffix *-al*. Thus, the structure is named pentanal. The correct structures associated with the other choices are

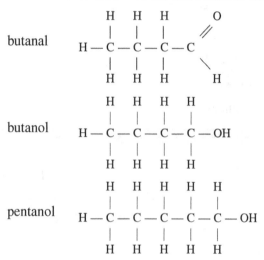

A–122

(B)   Consulting the periodic table, we find that sulfur (atomic number 16) has the electronic configuration

$$1s^2\, 2s^2\, 2p^6\, 3s^2\, 3p^4$$

Take Quiz 2 at the REA Study Center to test your immediate grasp of the topics in this section.

(www.rea.com/studycenter)

Section III

Quantitative Reasoning

DIRECTIONS: Each of the questions or incomplete statements in this section is followed by four suggested answers or completions. Select the one that is best in each case.

Questions

Q-1

What part of three-fourths is one-tenth?

(A) $\frac{1}{8}$

(B) $\frac{15}{2}$

(C) $\frac{2}{15}$

(D) $\frac{3}{40}$

Your Answer _____

$$\left(\frac{3}{4}\right)\left(\frac{1}{10}\right) = \frac{3}{40}$$

$2x + 12 - 9 = 3x$

$2x + 3 = 3x$

$3 = 3x - 2x$

$3 = 1x$

$x = 3$

Q-2

Find the value of x in $2x + 12 = 3x + 9$.

(A) 1

(B) 2

(C) 3

(D) 4

Your Answer _____

Answers

(C)   First, observe that three-fourths is $\frac{3}{4}$ and one-tenth is $\frac{1}{10}$. Let x be the unknown part which must be found. Then, one can write from the statement of the problem that the x part of three-fourths is given by

$$\frac{3}{4}x$$

The equation for the problem is given by $\frac{3}{4}x = \frac{1}{10}$. Multiplying both sides of the equation by the reciprocal of $\frac{3}{4}$, one obtains the following:

$$\left(\frac{4}{3}\right)\frac{3}{4}x = \left(\frac{4}{3}\right)\frac{1}{10} \text{ or } x = \frac{4}{30} \text{ or } x = \frac{2}{15}$$

which is choice (C).

Response (D) is obtained by incorrectly finding the product of $\frac{3}{4}$ and $\frac{1}{10}$ to be the unknown part. Response (B) is obtained by dividing $\frac{3}{4}$ by $\frac{1}{10}$.

A-2

(C)   Simplify $2x + 12 = 3x + 9$.

$$12 - 9 = 3x - 2x$$
$$3 = x$$

Questions

Q-3

Peter has five rulers of 30 cm each and three of 20 cm each. What is the average length of Peter's rulers?

(A) 25

(B) 27

(C) 23

(D) 26.25

Read!

$$\begin{array}{r} 30 \\ +20 \\ \hline 50 \end{array}$$

$\dfrac{50}{2} = 25$

Your Answer _____

Q-4

Two pounds of pears and one pound of peaches cost $1.40. Three pounds of pears and two pounds of peaches cost $2.40. How much is the combined cost of one pound of pears and one pound of peaches?

(A) $2.00

(B) $1.50

(C) $1.60

(D) $1.00

2 pears + 1 peach = 1.40

3 pears + 2 peach = 2.40

Your Answer _____

Answers

A–3

(D)   Average = $\dfrac{5 \times 30 + 3 \times 20}{8}$

Average = $\dfrac{150 + 60}{8} = \dfrac{210}{8} = 26.25$

A–4

(D)   Let x = cost of one pound of pears
Let y = cost of one pound of peaches
$2x + y = 1.4$
$3x + 2y = 2.4$
$4x + 2y = 2.8$
$3x + 2y = 2.4$
$x = .4$
$y = .6$
Therefore, $x + y = 1.00$

Questions

Q–5

One number is 2 more than 3 times another. Their sum is 22. Find the numbers.

(A) 8, 14

(B) 2, 20

(C) 5, 17

(D) 4, 18

Your Answer _____

_____

= 22

$4 \times 3 = 12$

$5 \times 3 = 15 + 2 = 17$ $\checkmark$ $17 + 5 = 22$

Most pharmacy graduates can expect to receive multiple job offers at the time of graduation. There is great potential for advancement and competitive salaries within a pharmacy career. (www.aacp.org)

Answers

A–5

(C)   Based on the information given in the first sentence of the problem, one needs to first represent the unknown numbers. So let x be a number. Then, the other number is given by $3x + 2$, which is two more than 3 times the first number. So the two numbers are x and $3x + 2$.

Next, form an equation by adding the two numbers and setting the sum equal to 22 and then solve the equation for the two numbers.

$$x + 3x + 2 = 22$$
$$4x + 2 = 22$$
$$4x = 20$$
$$x = 5, \text{ one of the numbers.}$$

The other number is given by

$$3x + 2 = 3(5) + 2 = 15 + 2 = 17, \text{ the other}$$
number.

Hence, answer choice (C) is correct. The other answer choices fail to satisfy the equation $x + 3x + 2 = 22$.

Questions

Q–6

Which of the following represents moving the graph of $y = x^2 - 8x + 15$ to the right three units and down two units?

(A) $y = x^2 + 5x + 13$

(B) $y = x^2 - 11x + 17$

(C) $y = x^2 + 3x - 2$

(D) $y = x^2 - 14x + 46$

Your Answer _____

_____

Increases in average life span and the increased incidence of chronic diseases as well as the increased complexity, number and sophistication of medications and related products point to a healthy future for a career in pharmacy. (www.aacp.org)

Answers

A–6

(D) $y = x^2 - 8x + 15$

We first put this equation into standard form by completing the square:

$$y = (x^2 - 8x + \underline{\quad}) + 15 - \underline{\quad}$$
$$y = (x^2 - 8x + \underline{16}) + 15 - \underline{16}$$
$$y = (x - 4)^2 - 1$$

To move three units to the right, and two units down, we will have

$$y = (x - 4 - 3)^2 - 1 - 2$$
$$y = (x - 7)^2 - 3$$

Multiplying this out, we have

$$y = x^2 - 14x + 49 - 3$$
$$y = x^2 - 14x + 46$$

Questions

Q–7

Find the equation of a circle in general form with center $(-1, -5)$ and tangent to the x-axis.

(A) $x^2 + y^2 + 2x + 10y + 1 = 0$

(B) $x^2 + y^2 - 2x - 10y + 1 = 0$

(C) $x^2 + y^2 + 2x + 10y + 25 = 0$

(D) $x^2 + y^2 - 2x - 10y - 25 = 0$

Your Answer _____

_____

1, 3, 5, 7, 9

Q–8

If n is the first of three consecutive odd numbers, which of the following represents the sum of the three numbers?

(A) $n + 2$

(B) $n + 4$

(C) $n + 6$

(D) $3n + 6$

$3(3) + 6$

$9 + 6 = 15$

$3 + 5 + 7 = 15$

Your Answer _____

_____

243

Answers

A-7

(A) Since the circle is tangent to the x-axis, the distance from the center to the x-axis is the radius, or 5 units. Using $(x - h)^2 + (y - k)^2 = r^2$, with $(h, k) = (-1, -5)$ and $r = 5$, we have

$$(x - (-1))^2 + (y - (-5))^2 = 5^2$$

$$(x + 1)^2 + (y + 5)^2 = 25$$

Multiplying this out, we have

$$x^2 + 2x + 1 + y^2 + 10y + 25 = 25$$

or

$$x^2 + y^2 + 2x + 10y + 1 = 0$$

A-8

(D) With n being the first odd number, it follows that $n + 2$ and $n + 4$ are the next two odd numbers. This eliminates answer choices (A) and (B) on the basis that each one of them represents only one of the two consecutive odd numbers that follow n. Since the sum of the three consecutive odd numbers is $n + (n + 2) + (n + 4) = 3n + 6$, it follows that answer choice (C) is incorrect, which leaves answer choice (D) as correct.

Questions

Q–9

A runner takes nine seconds to run a distance of 132 feet. What is the runner's speed in miles per hour?

(A) 9

(B) 10

(C) 11

(D) 12

$$\left(\frac{9\,sec}{132\,ft}\right)\left(\frac{1\,min}{60\,sec}\right)\left(\frac{1\,hr}{60\,min}\right)$$

$$\left(\frac{9\,hr}{475,200\,ft}\right)\left(\frac{1}{1\,mil}\right)$$

Your Answer _____

Q–10

35 is 7% of what quantity?

(A) 2.45

(B) 5

(C) 245

(D) 500

$$\frac{7}{35} \times \frac{100}{x}$$

$$3500 = 7x$$

$$x = 500$$

Your Answer _____

Answers

A–9

(B) First one must determine the equivalent of 132 ft./9 sec. in terms of miles/hour in order to solve the problem. Recall that 1 hour = 60 min. = 3,600 sec. and 1 mile = 5,280 ft. Thus, one can set up the following proportion:

$$\frac{132 \text{ ft}}{9 \text{ sec}} = \frac{x \text{ ft}}{1 \text{ hr}} = \frac{x \text{ ft}}{3,600 \text{ sec}}$$

and solve for x. The result is

$$\frac{9x \text{ ft}}{\text{sec}} = \frac{132(3,600) \text{ ft}}{\text{sec}}$$

$$x = \frac{475,200}{9} = 52,800 \text{ ft or 10 miles.}$$

Hence, the speed is 10 miles per hour.

A–10

(D) Let x = number

$$.07x = 35$$
$$x = 500$$
$$\frac{.07x}{.07} = \frac{35}{.07}$$

Therefore, the correct choice is (D).

Questions

Do I get a calc.?

Q–11

After taking four tests, Joan has an average grade of 79 points. What grade must she get on her fifth test to achieve an 83 point average?

(A) 83

(B) 86

(C) 87

(D) 99

$79 + 99 =$

Your Answer Not just a simple average $(4)\dfrac{79 + x}{5} = 83$

Q–12

Give the equations of the vertical asymptotes of the rational function

$$f(x) = \frac{x^2 + x - 2}{3x^2 - x - 10}$$

(A) $y = \dfrac{1}{3}$

(B) $y = 0$

(C) $x = 2, x = -\dfrac{5}{3}$

(D) $x = -2, x = \dfrac{5}{3}$

Your Answer _____

Answers

A–11

(D)   Let x = the score of Joan's last test

$$83 = \frac{4(79) + x}{5}$$

$$83(5) = 316 + x$$
$$415 - 316 = x$$
$$99 = x$$

A–12

(C) $$f(x) = \frac{x^2 + x - 2}{3x^2 - x - 10}$$

Vertical asymptotes occur where the denominator is equal to zero. We must also see whether there are "holes" in the graph, rather than vertical asymptotes, by checking for common variable factors in the numerator and denominator.

$$f(x) = \frac{(x-1)(x+2)}{(3x+5)(x-2)}$$

There are no holes in the graph, so we get the vertical asymptotes by setting each factor in the denominator equal to zero.

$$3x + 5 = 0 \qquad x - 2 = 0$$

$$x = -\frac{5}{3} \qquad x = 2$$

Questions

Q–13

x	-3	-2	1	4
$f(x)$	$-\dfrac{27}{2}$	-4	$\dfrac{1}{2}$	32

A power function can be defined as $f(x) = ax^p$, where a and p are constants. Using the values in the table above, find the value of a.

(A) $-\dfrac{1}{2}$

(B) $\dfrac{1}{2}$

(C) 2

(D) 3

$$5a(-2)^p = -4$$
$$5a(1) = -4$$
$$\frac{5a}{5} = \frac{-4}{5}$$
$$a =$$

Your Answer _____

Q–14

Solve the inequality $7 - 3x \le 19$.

(A) $x = 4$

(B) $x = -4$

(C) $x \ge -4$

(D) $x \le -4$

$$7 - 12 \le 19$$
$$-5 \le 19$$
$$7 + 12$$
$$19 \le 19$$

$$-\cancel{5}$$
$$7 + 15 \le 19$$
$$22 \le 19$$

Your Answer _____

Answers

A–13

(B) To solve this problem, we can use a calculator to define the power function that generated the table values. Without a calculator, we can substitute the x and y values from the table into the general formula and solve for a and p. For this problem, the easiest point to use is $\left(1, \dfrac{1}{2}\right)$ in the function.

$$f(x) = ax^p$$
$$\frac{1}{2} = a(1)^2$$
$$\frac{1}{2} = a$$

how do you know p is 2?

A–14

(C) Simplify

$7 - 3x \le 19$	Add -7 to both sides
$-3x \le 19 - 7$	Divide both sides by (-3).
$x \ge 12 \div (-3)$	The sense of the inequality
$x \ge -4$	changes when multiplied or divided by a negative number.

Questions

Q–15

A truck contains 150 small packages, some weighing 1 kg each and some weighing 2 kg each. How many packages weighing 2 kg each are in the truck if the total weight of all the packages is 264 kg?

(A) 36

(B) 52

(C) 88

(D) 114

Your Answer _____

_____

$$264 = 1x + 2x$$
$$264 = 3x$$
$$x = 88/150 = 0.5$$

Employment of pharmacists is expected to grow 25 percent for all occupations through 2020. (www.bls.gov)

Answers

(D) One way to attack this problem is to solve it algebraically.

Let x represent the number of packages weighing 2 kg each. Then $(150 - x)$ represents the number of packages weighing 1 kg each.

Therefore,

$$2x + 1(150 - x) = 264$$
$$2x + 150 - x = 264$$
$$x = 264 - 150$$
$$x = 114$$

Thus, there are 114 packages weighing 2 kg each on the truck.

Another way to solve this problem is to test each of the answer choices. Note that if, for example, the number of packages weighing 2 kg each is 36 (answer choice [A]), then the number of packages weighing 1 kg each will be $(150 - 36) = 114$. Testing the answer choices yields:

(A) $(36)(2) + (150 - 36)(1) = 72 + 114 = 186$
     (wrong)
(B) $(52)(2) + (150 - 52)(1) = 104 + 98 = 202$
     (wrong)
(C) $(88)(2) + (150-88)(1) = 176 + 62 = 238$
     (wrong)
(D) $(114)(2) + (150 - 114)(1) = 228 + 36 = 264$
     (correct)

Questions

Q–16

What is the period of $y = -4\sin\dfrac{x}{2}$?

(A) π

(B) $\dfrac{\pi}{4}$

(C) $\dfrac{\pi}{2}$

(D) 4π

Your Answer _____

_____

Q–17

A waitress's income consists of her salary and tips. Her salary is $150 a week. During one week that included a holiday, her tips were ⁵⁄₄ of her salary. What fraction of her income for the week came from tips?

(A) $\dfrac{5}{8}$

(B) $\dfrac{5}{4}$

(C) $\dfrac{4}{9}$

(D) $\dfrac{5}{9}$

$150\left(\dfrac{5}{4}\right) = 187.5$

1.8

slow down!

Your Answer ___So close to the answer
every time!___

Answers

A–16

(D) $y = -4\sin\dfrac{x}{2}$?

For a sinusoidal function, the general form is $y = A\sin(B(\theta - h)) + k$, and the period is $\dfrac{2\pi}{|B|}$. Therefore, the period of the given function is $\dfrac{2\pi}{\frac{1}{2}} = 4\pi$.

A–17

(D) Note that tips for the week were $\left(\dfrac{5}{4}\right)(150)$. Thus, the total income was as follows:

$$(1)(150) + \left(\dfrac{5}{4}\right)(150) = \left(\dfrac{4}{4}\right)(150) + \left(\dfrac{5}{4}\right)(150)$$

$$337.5 \qquad = \left(\dfrac{9}{4}\right)(150) \ \checkmark$$

Therefore, tips made up $\dfrac{\left(\dfrac{5}{4}\right)(150)}{\left(\dfrac{9}{4}\right)(150)} = \dfrac{\frac{5}{4}}{\frac{9}{4}} = \dfrac{5}{9}$ of her income.

Notice that one could figure out the total income in order to arrive at the solution; however, this would be a waste of time.

Questions

Q–18

Find the median for the following set of numbers:
16, 22, 18, 21, 17, 21, 19, and 21.

(A) 21.0

(B) 20.0

(C) 22.0

(D) 19.0

16, 17, 18, 19, 21, 21, 21, 22

Your Answer _____

Q–19

The number missing in the series, 2, 6, 12, 20, x,
42, 56,

(A) 36.

(B) 24.

(C) 30.

(D) 38.

30

4 6 8 10
12

Your Answer _____

Answers

A-18

(B) The median is the middle value in a set of an odd number of values or the average of the two middle values of a set of an even number of values. Rearrange the set from smallest to largest values:

16, 17, 18, 19, 21, 21, 21, and 22.

$$\frac{(19 + 21)}{2} = 20.$$

A-19

(C) The difference between the first two numbers is 4(6 − 2); the difference between the second and third numbers is 6(12 − 6), which is two more than the first difference; the difference between the third and fourth numbers is 8(20 − 12), which is two more than the second difference; the difference between the fourth and fifth numbers is 10(x − 20). Thus, the value of x is given by $x − 20 = 10$. Solving for x yields 30. So, the correct answer choice is (C).

Questions

Q-20

What is the factorization of $x^2 + ax - 2x - 2a$?

(A) $(x + 2)(x - a)$

(B) $(x - 2)(x + a)$

(C) $(x + 2)(x + a)$

(D) $(x - 2)(x - a)$

Your Answer _____

_____

$$x^2 - ay + 2y - 2a$$

$$x^2 + ax - 2y - 2a$$

Some pharmacists specialize in specific drug therapy areas, such as intravenous nutrition support, oncology, nuclear pharmacy, geriatric pharmacy and psychopharmacotherapy. (www.bls.gov)

Answers

(B) First, group the expression and then find the monomial factor for each group as follows:

$$(x^2 + ax) + (-2x - 2a) = x(x + a) + (-2)(x + a).$$

Then, the final factorization is formed by using $(x + a)$ and $(x - 2)$. So,

$$x^2 + ax - 2x - 2a = (x - 2)(x + a).$$

Notice that multiplying these two factors together will yield the original algebraic expression. So, (B) is the correct answer choice. The other answer choices are incorrect because when the factors are multiplied together in each case, the results do not yield the original algebraic expression.

Questions

Q–21

Jim is twice as old as Susan. If Jim were 4 years younger and Susan were 3 years older, their ages would differ by 12 years. What is the sum of their ages?

(A) 19

(B) 42

(C) 56

(D) 57

Your Answer _____

Jim = 2x   2x -1 =

Susan = y

Jim = x -4

Susan = x +3

About 21% of pharmacists worked part time in 2010. (www.bls.gov)

Answers

(D)   The easiest way to determine the result for this problem is to represent the unknown ages, set up an equation, and solve it. Begin by letting $x =$ age of Susan now. Then, $2x =$ the age of Jim now. The next step is to represent Jim's age 4 years ago and Susan's age 3 years from now. Thus, $2x - 4 =$ Jim's age 4 years ago. Then, $x + 3 =$ Susan's age 3 years from now. Finally, an equation can be set up by noting that the age represented by $2x - 4$ differs from the age represented by $x + 2$ by 12 years. So, the equation is given by the following:

$$(2x - 4) - (x + 3) = 12.$$

Solving for x one gets

$$2x - 4 - x - 3 = 12$$
$$x - 7 = 12$$
$$x - 7 + 7 = 12 + 7$$
$$x = 19, \text{ Susan's age now.}$$
$$2x = 38, \text{ Jim's age now.}$$

The sum of their ages $(19 + 38)$ is 57.

Questions

Q-22

Joe and Jim together have 14 marbles. Jim and Tim together have 10 marbles. Joe and Tim together have 12 marbles. What is the number of marbles that Tim has?

(A) 4
(B) 8
(C) 9
(D) 10

Your Answer ___Joe + Jim = 14___

___Jim + Tim = 10___

Joe + Tim = 12

$y = 10 - z$
$x = 12 - z$

$x + y = 14$
$y + z = 16$
$x + z = 12$

$(10 - z) + (12 - z) = 14$ $z = ?$
$10 - z + 12 - z = 14$ $22 - 2z = 14$
$8 = 2z$
$z = 4$

Q-23

Tom received 89, 94, 86, and 96 on the first four algebra tests. What grade must he receive on his last test to have an average of 92?

(A) 92 $89 + 94 + 86 + 96 +$
(B) 94
(C) 91
(D) 95

Your Answer _____

_____

Answers

A-22

(A) Let x = Joe's marbles, y = Jim's marbles, and z = Tim's marbles. It is given that

$x + y = 14$ (1)

$y + z = 10$ (2)

$x + z = 12$ (3)

Solve equation (2) for y and equation (3) for x. Then substitute their values in equation (1) and solve for z.

$$y + z = 10 \Rightarrow y + z - z = 10 - z \Rightarrow y = 10 - z$$

and

$$x + z = 12 \Rightarrow x + z - z = 12 - z \Rightarrow x = 12 - z$$

Thus,

$$x + y = 14 \Rightarrow (12 - z) + (10 - z) = 14$$
$$-2z + 22 = 14$$
$$-2z + 22 - 22 = 14 - 22$$
$$-2z = -8$$
$$z = 4, \text{Tim's marbles.}$$

A-23

(D) Let x = the grade of Tom's last test

$$\frac{89 + 94 + 86 + 96 + x}{5} = 92$$
$$89 + 94 + 86 + 96 + x = 92(5)$$
$$x = 460 - 365$$
$$x = 95$$

Questions

Q–24

$(5x - 3)(4x - 6) =$

(A) $20x^2 - 42x + 18$

(B) $20x^2 - 18$

(C) $20x^2 - 12x - 18$

(D) $30x^2 - 18$

Your Answer _____

_____

$$20x^2 - 30x - 12x + 18$$

$$20x^2 - 42x + 18$$

Q–25

Solve $|3 - 2x| = |5 - 4x|$ for x.

(A) 1

(B) $1, -\dfrac{4}{3}$

(C) $1, \dfrac{4}{3}$

(D) $-1, -\dfrac{4}{3}$

$$|3-2| = |5-4|$$

$$1 = 1$$

didn't
check
for
$\pm \dfrac{4}{3}$

Your Answer _____

_____

Answers

A–24

(A) $(5x - 3)(4x - 6) = 5x(4x - 6) - 3(4x - 6)$
$$= 20x^2 - 30x - 12x + 18$$
$$= 20x^2 - 42x + 18$$

A–25

(C) $|3 - 2x| = |5 - 4x|$

We must consider two cases.

Case 1

$3 - 2x = 5 - 4x$

$2x = 2$

$x = 1$

Case 2

$3 - 2x = -(5 - 4x)$

$3 - 2x = -5 + 4x$

$8 = 6x$ or $x = \dfrac{4}{3}$

Questions

Q–26

Which of the following equations can be used to find a number x, if the difference between the square of this number and 21 is the same as the product of 4 times the number?

(A) $x - 21 = 4x$

(B) $x^2 - 21 = 4x$

(C) $x^2 = 21 - 4x$

(D) $x + 4x^2 = 21$

Your Answer _____

_____

Most full-time salaried pharmacists work about 40 hours a week. (www.bls.gov)

Answers

(B) This problem can be easily solved by simply translating the English statements into algebraic expressions. "The difference between the square of this number, x, and 21" can be written as $x^2 - 21$. "Is the same as" means equal (=). "The product of 4 times the number" can be written as $4x$. Thus, the information in this problem can be written as follows:

$$x^2 - 21 = 4x.$$

Answer choice (A) is eliminated because the left-hand side of the equation, $x - 21 = 4x$, gives the difference between the number x and 21 and not the difference between the square of the number x and 21. Answer choice (C) is eliminated because it states that the difference between 21 and 4 times the number x is equal to the square of the number x. In addition, neither of the equations $x + 4x^2 = 21$ and $x^2 + 21 = 4x$ is equivalent to the equation $x^2 - 21 = 4x$, which was obtained by translating the English statements in this problem into algebraic expressions. Thus, answer choice (D) is also eliminated, leaving answer choice (B) as the only correct choice.

Q–27

Emile receives a flat weekly salary of $240 plus 12% commission of the total volume of all sales he makes. What must his dollar volume be in a week if he is to make a total weekly salary of $540?

(A) $2,880

(B) $3,600

(C) $6,480

(D) $2,500

Your Answer _____

_____

$$540$$
$$-240$$
$$\overline{300} = 12\%$$

$$.12x = 300$$

$$\frac{300}{.12} \times \frac{x}{1.00}$$

$$\frac{300}{.12} =$$

In 2016, about 58% of pharmacists worked in community pharmacies that are either independently owned or part of a drugstore chain, grocery store, department store, or mass merchandiser. (www.bls.gov)

Answers

(D) Since we do not know Emile's dollar volume during the week in question, we can assign this amount the value of x.

Now, Emile's total salary of $540 can be divided into two parts; one part is his flat salary of $240, and the other part is his salary from commissions, which amounts to $540 – $240 = $300. This part of his salary is equal to 12% of his dollar volume, x. Thus, 12% of x = $300. This means

$$(0.12)x = 300$$
$$x = 300/0.12 = \$2,500.$$

Another way to attack this problem is to test each answer choice as follows:

(A) (0.12) ($2,800) = $345.60 ≠ $300   (wrong)
(B) (0.12) ($3,600) = $432 ≠ $300   (wrong)
(C) (0.12) ($6,400) = $768 ≠ $300   (wrong)
(D) (0.12) ($2,500) = $300   (correct)

Questions

Q–28

In the Carco Auto Factory, robots assemble cars. If 3 robots assemble 17 cars in 10 minutes, how many cars can 14 robots assemble in 45 minutes if all robots work at the same rate all the time?

(A) 357

(B) 340

(C) 705

(D) 150

Your Answer _____

$$3 \rightarrow 17 \rightarrow 10 \qquad .566$$
$$14 \rightarrow \qquad \rightarrow 45$$

In 2016, about 25% of salaried pharmacists worked in hospitals. (www.bls.gov)

Answers

(A) One method for attacking this problem is to let x be the number of cars that 14 robots can assemble in 45 minutes. Because the robots work at the same rate all the time, we can express this rate by using the information that 3 robots can assemble 17 cars in 10 minutes.

Now, if 3 robots can assemble 17 cars in 10 minutes, then 3 robots can assemble $^{17}\!/_{10}$ cars in 1 minute. Consequently, 1 robot assembles $\frac{1}{3}(^{17}\!/_{10})$ or $^{17}\!/_{30}$ of a car in 1 minute.

Similarly, if 14 robots assemble x cars in 45 minutes, then the 14 robots assemble $^{x}\!/_{45}$ cars in 1 minute. Thus, 1 robot assembles $\frac{1}{14}(^{x}\!/_{45})$, or $^{x}\!/_{45(45)}$ of a car in 1 minute. Because the rates are equal, we have the proportion

$$30x = (630)(17)$$
$$= 10{,}710$$
$$x = \frac{10{,}710}{30} = 357$$

Solving this proportion for x yields

$$\frac{x}{14(45)} = \frac{17}{30}$$

$$\frac{x}{630} = \frac{17}{30}$$

Questions

Q–29

What is the median of the following group of scores?
27, 27, 26, 26, 26, 26, 18, 13, 36, 36, 30, 30, 30, 27, 29

(A) 30

(B) 26

(C) 25.4

(D) 27

Your Answer _____

13, 18, 26, 26, 26, 26, 27, 27, 27, 29, 30, 30, 30, 36, 36

Q–30

The solution of the equation $4 - 5(2y + 4) = 4$ is

(A) $-\frac{2}{5}$.

(B) 8.

(C) 4.

(D) -2.

$$4 - 10y - 20 = 4$$
$$-10y - 16 = 4$$
$$-10y = 20$$
$$y = -2$$

Your Answer _____

_____

Answers

A–29

(D) Choices (A), (B), and (C) are incorrect. This is not the median. The median is the middle value in a sequence of numbers when the numbers are arranged in ascending or descending order. (D) is correct. The median is the middle value in a sequence of numbers when the numbers are arranged in ascending or descending order. When this is done, 27 is the median value.

A–30

(D) Choices (A), (B), and (C) are incorrect. Try substituting the answer in the original equation. Simplify the equation. Remember that an equation can be multiplied, divided, subtracted, or added by the same number on both sides of the equal sign to help reduce it. (D) is correct.

$4 - 5(2y + 4) = 4$

$4 - 10y - 20 = 4$ On the left-hand side of the equation apply the distributive property.

$4 - 20 - 4 = 10y$ Add $10y$ and -4 to both sides of the equation to isolate the terms with y.

$-20 = 10y$

$-2 = y$ Divide both sides by 10.

Questions

Q–31

Mr. Smith goes to Lucky Duck Casino and in the first game he loses one-third of his money, in the second game he loses half of the rest. If he still has $1,000, how much money did he have when he arrived at the casino?

(A) $1,000

(B) $2,000

(C) $3,000

(D) $6,000

Your Answer _____

6,000   3,000

4,000   2,000

2,000   1,000

1,000

An aging population means more pharmacy services are required in nursing homes, assisted living facilities, and home care settings, where the most rapid job growth among pharmacists is expected. (www.bls.gov)

Answers

(C) (A) is incorrect. This answer is too small since this is the same amount that Mr. Smith had at the end and he had lost some in two games. Let $x =$ the amount of money that he arrived with at the casino. Then set up an equation that follows the given problem. Choices (B) and (D) are also incorrect. Read the problem carefully and make sure that the money lost is subtracted from the equation. Let $x =$ the amount of money that he arrived with at the casino. Then set up an equation that follows the given problem. (C) is correct. Let $x =$ the amount of money that he arrived with at the casino. Then set up an equation that follows the given problem. As follows:

$$x - \frac{1}{3}x = \frac{2}{3}x, \text{ the amount of money left after the first game.}$$

$$\frac{2}{3}x - \frac{1}{2}\left(\frac{2}{3}x\right) = \frac{1}{3}x, \text{ the amount of money left at the end.}$$

$$\$1{,}000 = \frac{1}{3}x, \text{ information given in the problem.}$$

$$x = \$3{,}000, \text{ the amount of money at the start.}$$

Q–32

Tickets for a particular concert cost $5 each if purchased in advance and $7 each if bought at the box office on the day of the concert. For this particular concert, 1,200 tickets were sold and the receipts were $6,700. How many tickets were bought at the box office on the day of the concert?

(A) 500

(B) 700

(C) 600

(D) 350

Your Answer _____

Median annual wage of pharmacists in 2016 was $122,230. (www.bls.gov)

Seen a similiar type questions!

Q15

Answers

A-32

(D) Choices (A), (B), and (C) are incorrect. Create an algebraic formula to find the number of tickets bought at the box office. Recheck the solution with the given information. (D) is correct. Let x be the number of tickets bought at the box office. Then the number of tickets purchased in advance equals $(1,200 - x)$. Set up the formula with the rest of the information as follows:

$$5(1,200 - x) + 7x = 6,700$$
$$6,000 - 5x + 7x = 6,700$$
$$2x = 6,700 - 6,000$$
$$2x = 700$$
$$x = 350$$

Questions

Q-33

If $2a + 2b = 1$, and $6a - 2b = 5$, which of the following statements is true?

(A) $3a - b = 5$

(B) $a + b > 3a - b$

(C) $a + b = -2$

(D) $a + b < 3a - b$

Your Answer _____

_____

$$2a + 2b = 1$$
$$2a + 2b - 1 = 0$$
$$6a - 2b - 5 = 0$$
$$2a + 2b - 1 = 6a - 2b - 5$$
$$4b - 1 = 4a - 5$$

Pharmacists usually work in clean, well-lit, and well-ventilated areas, and spend most of their workday on their feet. (www.bls.gov)

$$4b + 4 = 4a$$
$$4 = 4a - 4b$$
$$1 = a - b$$

Answers

(D) Choices (A), (B), and (C) are incorrect. Rewrite the equations and compare to the statements given. Be careful when simplifying. (D) is correct. One method to solve this problem is to rewrite the equations and compare the results.

$$2a + 2b = 1 \qquad \text{and} \qquad 6a - 2b = 5$$
$$2(a + b) = 1 \qquad\qquad\qquad 2(3a - b) = 5$$
$$(a + b) = \tfrac{1}{2} \qquad\qquad\qquad (3a - b) = \tfrac{5}{2}$$

Another method to solve this problem is to solve for a and b:

$$2a + 2b = 1$$
$$6a + 2b = 5$$
$$8a + 0b = 6$$
$$8a = 6$$
$$a = \frac{6}{8} = \frac{3}{4}$$
$$2\left(\frac{3}{4}\right) + 2b = 1$$
$$2b = 1 - 1\frac{1}{2}$$
$$2b = -\frac{1}{2}$$
$$b = -\frac{1}{4}$$

These numbers can then be substituted into the equation given.

Questions

Q–34

If $6x + 12 = 5$, then the value of $(x + 2)$ is

(A) $-{}^{19}\!/_6$

(B) $-1{}^1\!/_6$

(C) ${}^5\!/_6$

(D) $3{}^1\!/_6$

$6x = 7$

$x = \frac{7}{6}$

$\frac{7}{6} + \frac{12}{6} = \frac{19}{6}$

Your Answer _____

_____

Q–35

The most economical price among the following prices is

(A) 10 oz. for 16¢. $.62 \cdot 5$

(B) 2 oz. for 3¢. 66.6

(C) 4 oz. for 7¢. 57.14

(D) 20 oz. for 34¢.

1.6

1.5

1.75

1.7

Your Answer ___divide dollars by oz.___

_____

Answers

A–34

(C)   (C) is correct. One way to solve the problem is to find the value of x, then substitute it into $(x + 2)$. Another way is to factor the equation as

$$6x + 12 = 5$$
$$6(x + 2) = 5$$
$$(x + 2) = \tfrac{5}{6}.$$

This gives the answer directly.

   Choices (A), (B), and (D) are incorrect. Solve for x and find the value of $(x + 2)$.

A–35

(B)   Choices (A), (C), and (D) are incorrect. Find the price per ounce for the given prices. Compare the prices. (B) is correct. Divide each price by the number of ounces in each price to obtain the following prices per ounce for the given prices:

$$\frac{16}{10} \quad \frac{3}{2} \quad \frac{7}{4} \quad \frac{34}{20} \quad \frac{13}{8}$$

Then find the least common denominator, 40, to be able to compare the prices.

$$\frac{64}{40} \quad \frac{60}{40} \quad \frac{70}{40} \quad \frac{68}{40} \quad \frac{65}{40}$$

Since the smallest fraction is $^{60}/_{40}$, it follows that the most economical price among the given prices is 2 oz. for 3¢.

Questions

If *n* is an integer, which of the following represents an odd number?

(A) $2n + 3$

(B) $2n$

(C) $2n + 2$

(D) $3n$

Your Answer _____

_____

Answers

(A) (A) is correct. n can be an odd number or an even number. $2n$ is an even number and $2n + 3$ is odd because even + odd = odd. (B) is incorrect. n can be an odd number or an even number. $2n$ is always an even number. (C) is incorrect. n can be an odd number or an even number. $2n$ is an even number and $2n + 2$ is even because even + even = even. (D) is incorrect. n can be an odd number or an even number. When n is odd, $3n$ is odd (odd × odd = odd). But this is not true if n is an even number, since $3n$ is even (odd × even = even).

Questions

Q–37

A postal truck leaves its station and heads for Chicago, averaging 40 mph. An error in the mailing schedule is spotted and 24 minutes after the truck leaves, a car is sent to overtake the truck. If the car averages 50 mph, how long will it take to catch the postal truck?

(A) 2.6 hours

(B) 3 hours

(C) 2 hours

(D) 1.6 hours

Your Answer _____

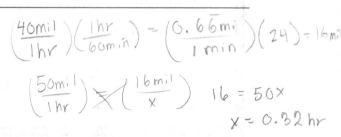

$$\left(\frac{40mil}{1hr}\right)\left(\frac{1hr}{60min}\right) = \left(\frac{0.6\overline{6}mi}{1min}\right)(24) = 16mi$$

$$\left(\frac{50mil}{1hr}\right) \neq \left(\frac{16mil}{x}\right) \quad 16 = 50x$$

$$x = 0.32\ hr$$

In 1546, the first pharmacopoeia (list of drugs and their preparation) appeared in Germany. (Encyclopedia Britannica, 2017.)

Answers

(D) Choices (A), (B), and (C) are incorrect. Use Distance = Rate × Time and set up an algebraic equation to solve for the time. Let t be the time, in hours, it takes the car to catch up with the postal truck. Then the time of travel of the truck should be $(t + 24/60)$ hours. (D) is correct. Use Distance = Rate × Time and set up an algebraic equation to solve for the time. Let t be the time, in hours, it takes the car to catch up with the postal truck. Then the time of travel of the truck should be $(t + 24/60)$ hours.

Using the distance formula:

Truck: $d_t = 40(t + 0.4)$
$= 40t + 16$

Car: $d_c = 50t$

But the distance traveled by the truck and car will be the same, so

$$d_t = d_c$$
$$40t + 16 = 50t$$
$$16 = 10t$$
$$t = 1.6$$

Thus, it takes the car 1.6 hours to catch up with the postal truck.

Questions

Q–38

If $b = 6a - 2bx$, $a = 9$ and $b = 6$, then $x =$

(A) 2.

(B) 0.

(C) 1.

(D) 4.

$6 = 6(9) - 2(6)x$

$6 = 54 - 12x$

$12x = 48$

$x = 4$

Your Answer _____

Q–39

In a class of 40 students, 30 speak French and 20 speak German. What is the lowest possible number of students who speak both languages?

(A) 5

(B) 20

(C) 15

(D) 10

$30 \quad 20$

Your Answer _____

Answers

(D) Choices (A), (B), and (C) are incorrect. Insert the values of a and b into the expression to solve for x. The value of $a = 9$ and the value of $b = 6$. (D) is correct. If $b = 6a - 2bx$, then

$$6 = (6 \times 9) - [2 \times 6 \times (x)] = 54 - 12x$$
$$12x = 54 - 6 = 48$$
$$x = 4$$

(D) Choices (A), (B), and (C) are incorrect. Set up an algebraic problem with x = the students who speak both French and German. Total class = students who speak only French + students who speak only German + students who speak both French and German. (D) is correct. Set up an algebraic problem with x = the students who speak both French and German.

Therefore, the number of students who speak only French = $30 - x$

and the number of students who speak only German = $20 - x$

Total class = students who speak only French + students who speak only German + students who speak both French and German.

Questions

Q–40

A man who is 40 years old has three sons, ages 6, 3, and 1. In how many years will the combined age of his three sons equal 80% of his age?

(A) 5

(B) 10

(C) 15

(D) 20

Your Answer _____

$$\frac{40}{100} = \frac{x}{80} \qquad 32$$

Q–41

One wall being made entirely of bricks is 40 percent built. If we need 1,200 more bricks to complete the wall, how many bricks will the wall have?

(A) 1,500

(B) 1,800

(C) 2,000

(D) 2,400

$$\frac{1,200 + x}{100} = \frac{x}{40} \times 40$$

$$100x = 48,006 + 46x$$

$$66x = 48,000$$

$$x = 800$$

Your Answer _____

Answers

(B)   Choices (A), (C), and (D) are incorrect. Let n = the number of years until the combined age of the sons equals 80% of the father's age. Remember to add n to each age. (B) is correct. Let n = the number of years until the combined age of the sons equals 80% of the father's age.

Their ages will be

      father = $40 + n$

      son #1 = $6 + n$

      son #2 = $3 + n$

      son #3 = $1 + n$.

Therefore,

$$(6 + n) + (3 + n) + (1 + n) = .80(40 + n)$$
$$10 + 3n = 32 + .8n$$
$$2.2n = 22$$
$$n = 10$$

A–41

(C)   If 40% of the bricks is already put in the wall and we need 1,200 more, then 1,200 bricks = 60% of the total bricks. Letting

$$x = \text{total bricks},$$
$$1,200 = \frac{60x}{100}$$
$$x = \frac{12,000}{6}$$
$$x = 2,000$$

Questions

Q–42

What percent of 260 is 13?

(A) .05%

(B) 5%

(C) 50%

(D) .5%

Your Answer _____

$$\frac{260}{100} = \frac{13}{x}$$

Q–43

Which of the following numbers is the smallest?

(A) −.6

(B) −.66

(C) $\frac{-2}{3}$ − .$\overline{66}$

(D) $\frac{-666}{1,000}$ −.666

Your Answer _____

Answers

A–42

(B)   In order to find what percent of 260 is 13, one needs only to form the following equation:

$$x\%(260) = 13$$

$$\frac{x(260)}{100} = 13$$

$$260x = 13(100)$$

$$x = \frac{1,300}{260} = 5\%$$

A–43

(C)   If we express all the numbers as decimals, we have

(A) –.6000
(B) –.6600
(C) $-.\overline{6}$ = –.6666...
(D) –.6660

Questions

Q–44

Which of the following has the smallest value?

(A) $\frac{1}{0.2}$ 5

(B) $\frac{0.1}{2}$ .05

(C) $\frac{0.2}{1}$ .2

(D) $\frac{0.2}{0.1}$ 2

Your Answer _____

_____

Q–45

What is the smallest positive number that leaves a remainder of 2 when the number is divided by 3, 4, or 5?

(A) 22

(B) 42

(C) 62

(D) 122

Your Answer _____

_____

Answers

A-44

(B)

Note that $\frac{.1}{2} = \frac{.1 \times 10}{2 \times 10} = \frac{1}{20}$ for response (B)

For choice (A), $\frac{1}{.2} = \frac{1 \times 10}{.2 \times 10} = \frac{10}{2} = 5$

which is larger than $\frac{1}{20}$.

For choice (C), $\frac{.2}{1} = \frac{.2 \times 10}{1 \times 10} = \frac{2}{10} = \frac{1}{5}$

which is larger than $\frac{1}{20}$.

For choice (D), $\frac{.2}{.1} = \frac{.2 \times 10}{.1 \times 10} = \frac{2}{1} = 2$

which is larger than $\frac{1}{20}$.

A-45

(C) First find the least common multiple (LCM) of 3, 4, and 5, which is simply $3 \times 4 \times 5 = 60$. Since 3 divides into 60, 4 divides into 60, and 5 divides into 60, then one needs only to add 2 to 60 in order to guarantee that the remainder in each case will be 2 when 3, 4, and 5, respectively, are divided into 62.

Q–46

Suppose the average of two numbers is *WX*. If the first number is *X*, what is the other number?

(A) *WX* – *X*

(B) 2*WX* – *W*

(C) *W*

(D) 2*WX* – *X*

Your Answer _____

_____

21   22

7, 9, 11
27   9, 11, 13   26   1, 3, 5
33 11, 13, 15   3, 5, 7
                       5, 7, 9

Q–47

Three times the first of three consecutive odd integers is three more than twice the third. What is the second of the three consecutive odd integers?

(A) 7

(B) 9

(C) 11

(D) 13

Your Answer _____

_____

Answers

A–46

(D)   Since X is the first number, then let y represent the second number in the average of two numbers. Thus, from what is given in the problem, one can write:

$$\frac{X+y}{2} = WX,$$

the average. Solving for y gives the other number. Hence,

$$X + y = 2WX$$
$$y = 2WX - X,$$

the second number.

A–47

(D)   Let x = the first odd integer, $x + 2$ = the second consecutive odd integer, and $x + 4$ = the third consecutive odd integer. Then, the following equation can be written based on what is given in the problem. Solve the equation.

$$3x = 2(x + 4) + 3$$
$$3x = 2x + 8 + 3$$
$$3x - 2x = 11$$
$$x = 11,$$

the first odd integer.

So, the second consecutive odd integer is $x + 2 = 11 + 2 = 13$.

Questions

Q–48

Jay and his brother Ray own a janitorial service. Jay can do a cleaning job alone in 5 hours and Ray can do the same job in 4 hours. How long will it take them to do the cleaning job together?

(A)   5 hours

(B)   1 hour

(C)   4 hours

(D) $2\frac{2}{9}$ hours

Your Answer _____

_____

$$\frac{1 \text{ job}}{5 \text{ hrs}} = 0.2$$

$$\frac{1 \text{ job}}{4 \text{ hrs}} = 0.25$$

Among the earliest modern pharmaceuticals were anesthetics such as morphine (1804); ether (1842); quinine (1820); and cocaine (1860). (Encyclopedia Britannica, 2017.)

Answers

(D) The traditional way to solve this problem is to set up and solve an equation. Consider what part of the job could be done in 1 hour by each person. Thus, Jay could do $\frac{1}{5}$ of the job in 1 hour and Ray could do $\frac{1}{4}$ of the job in the same amount of time. What is unknown is the part of the job they could do together in 1 hour, which can be represented by $\frac{1}{x}$. The x represents the amount of time the brothers can do the job together.

The sum of the amount of the job each brother can do in 1 hour equals the amount of the job they can do together in 1 hour. Hence, the equation is given by:

$$\frac{1}{5} + \frac{1}{4} = \frac{1}{x}$$

Solving for x you calculate as follows:

$$\frac{1}{5} \times \frac{4}{4} + \frac{1}{4} \times \frac{5}{5} = \frac{1}{x}$$

Side Notes

$$\frac{4}{20} + \frac{5}{20} = \frac{1}{x}$$
1) Find the LCD.
2) Add like fractions on left side of the equation.

$$\frac{9}{20} = \frac{1}{x}$$
3) Cross multiply.

$$9x = 20$$

$$\frac{9x}{9} = \frac{20}{9}$$
4) Divide by 9 on both sides of the equation.

$$x = \frac{20}{9} \text{ or } 2\frac{2}{9} \text{ hours.}$$

To understand why answer choices (A) and (C) are incorrect one should consider another approach to the solution of the problem. The approach is referred to as a "logical" or "reasonable" method.

(Continued)

A–48 (Continued)

It is logical to believe that since Ray can complete the job in 4 hours by himself, he should finish the job in less than 4 hours with the help of his brother. Hence, answer choice (A) cannot be correct. Finally, answer choice (B), 1 hour, is also incorrect. To see this, one needs to assume for a moment that Jay could also do the cleaning job in 4 hours rather than the required 5 hours. Then together the brothers should be able to complete the job in one-half of the time or just 2 hours. Thus, it is logical that answer choice (B) does not represent enough time for both to do the job using the assumption.

Questions

Q–49

A box contains 6 red marbles and 4 blue marbles. What is the probability that if 2 marbles are simultaneously drawn from the box, both will be red?

(A) $\frac{2}{3}$

(B) $\frac{1}{3}$

(C) $\frac{1}{2}$

(D) $\frac{1}{5}$

Your Answer _____

_____

$$\left(\frac{6}{10}\right)\left(\frac{6}{10}\right)$$

Q–50

If $x - (4x - 8) + 9 + (6x - 8) = 9 - x + 24$, then $x =$

(A) 4.

(B) 2.

(C) 8.

(D) 6.

$$x - 4x + 8 + 9 + 6x - 8 = 9 - x + 24$$
$$3x + 9 = 9 - x + 24$$
$$4x = 24$$
$$x = 6$$

Your Answer _____

_____

Answers

A–49

(B) First find the number of different ways of drawing two marbles from the box. Use the permutation formula as follows:

$$P(10,2) = \frac{10!}{(10-2)!} = \frac{10!}{8!} = \frac{10(9)(8!)}{8!}$$

$$= 10(9) = 90 \text{ ways.}$$

Then find the number of different ways of drawing two red marbles from the box. Use the permutation formula as follows:

$$P(6, 2) = \frac{6!}{(6-2)!} = \frac{6!}{4!} = \frac{6(5)\,(4!)}{4!}$$

$$= 6(5) = 30 \text{ ways.}$$

Finally, to get the probability, form a ratio of P(6, 2) to P(10, 2). One gets the following:

The probability of drawing two red marbles from the box = $^{30}/_{90} = ^1/_3$.

A–50

(D) The most direct way to solve this problem is to perform the indicated operations in the given equation and solve it for x. Thus,

$$x - (4x - 8) + 9 + (6x - 8) = 9 - x + 24$$
$$x - 4x + 8 + 9 + 6x - 8 = 9 - x + 24$$
$$(x + 6x - 4x) + (8 - 8 + 9) = (9 + 24) - x$$
$$(7x - 4x) + 9 = 33 - x$$
$$3x + x = 33 - 9$$
$$4x = 24$$
$$x = 6$$

Questions

Q–51

If x and y are two different real numbers and $xz = yz$, then what is the value of z?

(A) $x - y$

(B) 1

(C) $\frac{x}{y}$

(D) 0

Your Answer _____

_____

Q–52

If it takes s sacks of grain to feed c chickens, how many sacks of grain are needed to feed k chickens?

(A) $\frac{ck}{s}$

(B) $\frac{k}{cs}$

(C) $\frac{cs}{k}$

(D) $\frac{sk}{c}$

$s \cdot c = s \cdot k$

Your Answer _____

_____

Answers

A–51

(D) Observe that $xz = yz$ implies that $x = y$ if z is not 0. But x and y are two different real numbers according to the original assumption in the problem. So, the only possible way for the equality to hold is for z to have a value of 0.

A–52

(D) Obviously, the more (less) chickens we have, the more (less) sacks of grain needed. Thus, this problem can be solved by using a direct proportion as follows:

$$\frac{\text{Number of sacks of feed } x}{\text{Number of chickens } x}$$

$$\frac{\text{Number of sacks of feed } y}{\text{Number of chickens } y}$$

Since it takes s sacks of grain to feed c chickens it follows that the correct proportion to use is

$$\frac{s}{c} = \frac{y}{k}$$

where y is the required number of sacks of grain needed to feed k chickens. Solving this proportion for y in terms of s, c, and k yields

$$\frac{s}{c} = \frac{y}{k}$$
$$cy = sk$$
$$y = \frac{sk}{c}$$

Questions

Q–53

Tilda's car gets 34 miles per gallon of gasoline and Naomi's car gets 8 miles per gallon. When traveling from Washington, D.C., to Philadelphia, they both used a whole number of gallons of gasoline. How far is it from Washington, D.C., to Philadelphia?

(A)   21 miles

(B)   32 miles

(C)   68 miles

(D)   136 miles

Your Answer _____

$$\frac{21}{34} \qquad \frac{21}{8} \qquad \frac{32}{34} \qquad \frac{32}{8}$$

$$\frac{68}{34} \qquad \frac{68}{8} \qquad \frac{136}{34} \qquad \frac{136}{8}$$

Pharmacology is the study of the interaction of drugs with living systems.
It is an essential component in the study of pharmacy. (www.aacp.org)

Answers

(D)   Tilda's car gets 34 miles per gallon of gasoline, and Naomi's car gets eight miles per gallon. Since each of them used a whole number of gallons of gasoline while traveling from Washington, D.C., to Philadelphia, it follows that the distance between the two cities must be a multiple of the two numbers 34 and 8.

The least common multiple of two (or more) whole numbers is the smallest non-zero whole number that is a multiple of both (all) of the numbers.

The least common multiple of 34 and 8 can be found by factoring each of 34 and 8 into their prime factors expressed in exponential form as follows:

$$8 = 2 \times 2 \times 2 = 2^3$$
$$34 = 2 \times 17$$

Then the least common multiple of 34 and 8 is equal to $2^3 \times 17 = 136$.

Another procedure for finding the least common multiple of two whole numbers is called the intersection-of-sets method. First, find the set of all positive multiples of both numbers, then find the set of all common multiples of both numbers, and, finally, pick the least element in the set.

In this problem, multiples of 8 are

8, 16, 24, 32, 40, 48, 56, 64, 72, 80, 88, 96, 104, 112, 120, 128, 136, 144, 152, 160, 168, …

Multiples of 34 are

34, 68, 102, 136, 170, …

The intersection of the multiples of 8 and 34 is the set

{136, 272, 408, …}

Because 136 is the least common multiple of 34 and 8, the distance from Washington, D.C., to Philadelphia is 136 miles.

(Continued)

Answers

A–53 (Continued)

Yet another way to attack this problem is to check if any of the answer choices is a common multiple of both 34 and 8.

(A) 21 is not a multiple of 34 or 8.
(B) 32 is a multiple of 8, but not of 34.
(C) 68 is a multiple of 34, but not of 8.
(D) 136 is a multiple of both 34 and 8.

Questions

Q–54

If *m* and *n* are consecutive integers, and *m* < *n*, which one of the following statements is always true?

(A) *n* – *m* is even.

(B) *m* must be odd.

(C) $m^2 + n^2$ is even.

(D) $n^2 – m^2$ is odd.

$4 + 9 = 13$

$9 - 4 = 5$

$m = 2 \quad n = 3$

$3 - 2 = 1$

$m = 3 \quad n = 4$

$4 - 3 = 1$

$9 + 16 = 25$

$16 - 9 = 5$

Your Answer _____

Pharmoeconomics is a branch of economics that applies cost-benefit, cost-effectiveness, cost-minimization, and cost-utility analyses to compare the economics of different pharmaceutical products or to compare drug therapy to other treatments. (www.aacp.org)

Answers

(D)   If m and n are consecutive integers, and $m < n$, it follows that

$$n = m + 1$$

Now, we can check each of the answer choices (A) through (D) as follows:

(A) $n - m = (m + 1) - m = m + 1 - m = 1$, which is odd. Thus, the statement in answer choice (A) is false.

(B) Since no specific information is given about the integer m, m can be an odd integer or an even integer. So, the statement in answer choice (B) is false.

(C) $m^2 + n^2 = m^2 + (m + 1)^2 = m^2 + m^2 + 2m + 1$
$$= 2m^2 + 2m + 1$$
$$= 2(m^2 + m) + 1$$

Since 2 times any integer (even or odd) yields an even integer, it follows that $2(m^2 + m)$ is an even integer, and hence, $2(m^2 + m) + 1$ is an odd integer. Hence, the statement in answer choice (C) is false.

(D) $n^2 - m^2 = (m + 1)^2 - m^2 = m^2 + 2m + 1 - m^2$
$$= 2m + 1$$

Again, since 2 times any integer (even or odd) yields an even integer, it follows that $2m$ is an even integer and $2m + 1$ is always an odd integer. Hence, the statement in answer choice (D) is correct.

Questions

Q–55

Pete and Lynn travel on bicycles from the same place, in opposite directions, Pete traveling 4 mph faster than Lynn. After 5 hours, they are 120 miles apart. What is Lynn's rate of travel?

(A)   20 mph

(B)   9 mph

(C)   10 mph

(D)   12 mph

Your Answer _____

_____

$$P = X + 4$$

$$L = X \qquad X + 4 + X = 120$$
$$2X = 116$$
$$X = \frac{58}{5} =$$

Pharmacogenomics is the science of understanding the correlation between an individual patient's genetic make-up (genotype) and their response to drug treatment. (www. aacp.org)

Answers

A-55

(C) Certainly, the easiest and the most direct way to answer this question is to translate the given information into an algebraic equation in one unknown variable, then solve it for that variable.

In this problem, the distance traveled, the time of travel, and the rate of travel are involved. The relationship between these three quantities is given by

$$\text{Distance} = \text{Rate} \times \text{Time}$$

So, let r be Lynn's rate of travel in miles per hour. Then Pete's rate of travel will be $(r + 4)$ miles per hour. After 5 hours of travel, the distance traveled by

Pete is $d_1 = \text{Rate} \times \text{Time}$
$$= (r + 4)\,5 = (5r + 20) \text{ miles}$$
Lynn is $d_2 = \text{Rate} \times \text{Time}$
$$= r(5) = 5r \text{ miles}$$

Since they are traveling in opposite directions, the total distance, d, traveled by both is equal to the sum of the distances traveled by both. A diagram, such as illustrated below, is helpful.

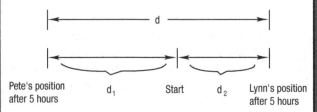

Pete's position after 5 hours · d_1 · Start · d_2 · Lynn's position after 5 hours

Now, total distance after 5 hours of travel is
$$\begin{aligned} d &= d_1 + d_2 \\ &= (5r + 20) + 5r \\ &= 5r + 20 + 5r \\ &= 10r + 20 \\ 120 &= 10r + 20 \\ 100 &= 10r \\ 10 &= r \end{aligned}$$

Q–56

$\frac{x+y}{y} = a; \frac{y}{x} =$

(A) 1

(B) a

(C) $\frac{1}{a}$

(D) $\frac{1}{(a-1)}$

$$\frac{x+y}{y} = a$$

$$x + y = ay$$

$$x = ay - y$$

$$x = y(a-1)$$

Your Answer _____

_____

Q–57

Jim filled $2/3$ of his swimming pool with 1,800 ft³ of water. What is the total capacity of Jim's swimming pool?

(A) 2,400 ft³

(B) 2,700 ft³

(C) 3,000 ft³

(D) 3,600 ft³

$$\frac{2}{3} = 1,800/_2$$

Your Answer _____

_____

Answers

A–56

(D) What is an expression for y as a function of a if $\frac{x+y}{y} = a$?

$$\frac{x+y}{y} = a$$

$$\frac{x}{y} + \frac{y}{y} = a$$

$$\frac{x}{y} + 1 = a$$

$$\frac{x}{y} = a - 1$$

$$\frac{y}{x} = \frac{1}{a-1}$$

A–57

(B) Let x be the total capacity of the swimming pool, then $\frac{2}{3} x$

$$x = \frac{1,800 \times 3}{2} = 2,700 \text{ ft}^3$$

The correct answer is (B).

Questions

Q–58

One year ago Pat was three times his sister's age. Next year he will be only twice her age. How old will Pat be in five more years?

(A) 8

(B) 12

(C) 11

(D) 13

Your Answer _____

$$11 - 5 = 6 \qquad 12 - 5 = 7 \qquad 13 - 5 = 8$$

$$3x = \qquad 3 \times 2 = 6$$

Q–59

Which of the following integers is the square of an integer for every integer x?

(A) $x^2 + x$

(B) $x^2 + 1$

(C) $x^2 + 2x$

(D) $x^2 + 2x + 1$

Your Answer _____

313

Answers

A–58

(B)

	Past	Present	Future
Pat	$x - 1$	x	$x + 1$
Sister	$y - 1$	y	$y + 1$

One year ago...
$$x - 1 = 3(y - 1)$$
Next year...
$$x + 1 = 2(y + 1)$$
$$x = 7$$
$$y = 3$$
Pat will be 12 years old in five more years.

A–59

(D) If $x = 1$ then response (B) is 2, response (A) is 2, and response (C) is 3. Thus, response (D) is the only response possible. Notice that by factoring the expression one gets
$$x^2 + 2x + 1 = (x + 1)(x + 1) = (x + 1)^2$$
which is the square of an integer for every integer x.

Questions

Q–60

What is the value(s) of x in the equation $(4x - 3)^2 = 4$?

(A) $\frac{5}{4}$

(B) $\frac{1}{4}$

(C) $\frac{5}{4}, \frac{1}{4}$

(D) $\frac{1}{2}, \frac{5}{2}$

Your Answer _____

$$(4x-3)(4x-3) = 4$$

$$16x^2 - 12x - 12x + 9 = 4$$

$$16x^2 - 24x + 5 = 0$$

$$\sqrt{(4x-3)^2} = \sqrt{4}$$

$$4x - 3 = 2$$

$$4x = 5$$

$$x = \frac{5}{4}$$

$$\pm\sqrt{}$$

Pharmaceutics is a discipline in the health sciences that is concerned with the design, development and rational use of medications for the treatment and prevention of disease. (www.aacp.org)

Answers

(C)   Take the square root of both sides of the equation to form two first equations and solve each for x as follows:

$$\sqrt{(4x-3)^2} = \sqrt{4} \qquad\qquad \sqrt{(4x-3)^2} = -\sqrt{4}$$
$$4x-3 = 2 \qquad\qquad\qquad 4x-3 = -2$$
$$4x = 2+3 \qquad \text{and} \qquad 4x = -2+3$$
$$x = \tfrac{5}{4} \qquad\qquad\qquad\qquad x = \tfrac{1}{4}$$

Hence, the values of x are $\tfrac{5}{4}$ and $\tfrac{1}{4}$, respectively, which is answer choice (C). Notice also that answer choices (A) and (B) each satisfy the original equation, but two values of x are required since the equation is quadratic.

Questions

Q–61

Simplify the following expression: $6 + 2(x - 4)$.

(A) $4x - 16$

(B) $2x - 14$

(C) $2x - 2$

(D) $-24x$

Your Answer _____

_____

$6 + 2x - 8$

$2x - 2$

Q–62

If six cans of beans cost $1.50, what is the price of eight cans of beans?

(A) $.90

(B) $1.00

.25 each

(C) $1.60

(D) $2.00

Your Answer _____

_____

Answers

A–61

(C)   When simplifying algebraic expressions, always work from left to right. First perform all multiplications and divisions then once this is done, start again from the left and do all additions and subtractions.

SUGGESTION: It can be helpful to translate the algebraic statement to English. For example, $6 + 2(x - 4)$ is "six plus two times the quantity x minus 4." The word "times" indicates multiplication, so we must first perform $2(x - 4)$ by using the distributive property $a(b - c) = ab - ac$:

$6 + 2(x - 4) = 6 + 2 \times x - 2 \times 4 = 6 + 2x - 8.$

Then we perform the subtraction to combine the terms 6 and 8:

$6 + 2x - 8 = 2x + (6 - 8) = 2x - 2.$

Note that we did not combine the $2x$ term with the other terms. This is because they are not like terms. Like terms are terms that have the same variables (with the same exponents). Since the terms 6 and 8 have no variable x, they are not like terms with $2x$.

A–62

(D)   Let x be the cost of one can of beans. Then $6x$ is the cost of six cans of beans. So $6x = \$1.50$. Dividing both sides of the equation by 6, we get $x = \$.25$ and, hence, since $8x$ is the cost of eight cans of beans, we have

$8x = 8 \times \$.25 = \$2.00.$

Questions

Q–63

Bonnie's average score on three tests is 71. Her first two test scores are 64 and 87. What is her score on the third test?

$64 + 87 +$

(A) 62

(B) 71

(C) 74

(D) 151

Your Answer _____

Q–64

A jar contains 20 balls. These balls are labeled 1 through 20. What is the probability that a ball chosen from the jar has a number on it which is divisible by 4?

$20, 16, 12, 8, 4$

(A) $\frac{1}{20}$

(B) $\frac{1}{5}$

(C) $\frac{1}{4}$

(D) 4

$\frac{5}{20} = \frac{1}{4}$

Your Answer _____

Answers

A–63

(A) Let t_1, t_2, and t_3 represent Bonnie's scores on tests one, two, and three, respectively. Then the equation representing Bonnie's average score is

$$\frac{t_1 + t_2 + t_3}{3} = 71.$$

We know that $t_1 = 64$ and $t_2 = 87$. Substitute this information into the equation above:

$$\frac{64 + 87 + t_3}{3} = 71.$$

Combining 64 and 87 and then multiplying both sides of the equation by 3 gives us

$$3 \times \frac{151 + t_3}{3} = 3 \times 71$$

$$\text{or } 151 + t_3 = 213.$$

Now subtract 151 from both sides of the equation so that

$$t_3 = 213 - 151 = 62.$$

A–64

(C) Note that the numbers 4, 8, 12, 16, and 20 are the only numbers from 1 through 20 that are divisible by 4. The probability that a ball chosen from the jar has a number on it that is divisible by 4 is given by

$$\frac{\text{total number of balls with numbers that are divisible by 4}}{\text{total number of possible outcomes}}$$

$$= \frac{5}{20} = \frac{1}{4}$$

Questions

Q-65

If $2x^2 + 5x - 3 = 0$ and $x > 0$, then what is the value of x?

(A) $-\frac{1}{2}$

(B) $\frac{1}{2}$

(C) 1

(D) $\frac{3}{2}$

Your Answer _____

_____

$x = 1$

$2 + 5 - 3 = 0$

4

Q-66

How many odd prime numbers are there between 1 and 20?

(A) 7

(B) 8

(C) 9

(D) 10

Your Answer _____

_____

Answers

A–65

(B) To solve the equation
$$2x^2 + 5x - 3 = 0,$$
we can factor the left side of the equation to get
$$(2x - 1)(x + 3) = 0.$$
Then use the following rule (this rule is sometimes called the Zero Product Property): If $a \times b = 0$, then either $a = 0$ or $b = 0$. Applying this to our problem gives us
$$2x - 1 = 0 \text{ or } x + 3 = 0.$$
Solve these two equations:
$$2x - 1 = 0 \rightarrow 2x = 1 \rightarrow x = \tfrac{1}{2}$$
$$x + 3 = 0 \rightarrow x = -3.$$
But $x > 0$, so $x = \tfrac{1}{2}$.

A–66

(A) A prime number is an integer that is greater than one and that has no integer divisors other than 1 and itself. So, the prime numbers between 1 and 20 (not including 1 and 20) are: 2, 3, 5, 7, 11, 13, 17, 19. But 2 is not an odd number, so the odd primes between 1 and 20 are: 3, 5, 7, 11, 13, 17, 19. Hence, there are seven odd primes between 1 and 20.

Questions

Q–67

Solve the following inequality for x: $8 - 2x \leq 10$.

(A) $x \leq 1$

(B) $x \geq -9$

(C) $x \leq -1$

(D) $x \geq -1$

Your Answer _____

$$8 - 2x \leq 10$$
$$-2x \leq 2$$
$$x \leq -1$$

Q–68

The ratio of men to women at University X is 3:7. If there are 6,153 women at University X, how many men are at University X?

(A) 879

(B) 1,895

(C) 2,051

(D) 2,637

$$\frac{3}{7} \times \frac{6,153}{x} \leftarrow \text{flip flop}$$

$$3x =$$

Your Answer _____

read Carefully!

Answers

Rules to remember...

A–67

(D)   To solve this inequality, we shall use the following rules:

>   (i) If $a \leq b$ and c is any number, then $a + c \leq b + c$.
>
>   (ii) If $a \leq b$ and $c < 0$, then $ca \geq cb$.

The goal in solving inequalities, as in solving equalities, is to change the inequality so that the variable is isolated (i.e., by itself on one side). So, in the equation $8 - 2x \leq 10$, we want the term $-2x$ by itself. To achieve this, use rule (i) above and add -8 to both sides obtaining

$$8 - 2x + (-8) \leq 10 + (-8)$$

or $-2x \leq 2$.

Now we use rule (ii) and multiply both sides of the inequality by $-\frac{1}{2}$ as follows:

$$-\frac{1}{2} \times 2x \geq -\frac{1}{2} \times 2$$

or $x \geq -1$.

A–68

(D)   Let m = the number of men at University X. Then we have the following proportion:

$$\frac{3}{7} = \frac{m}{6,153}$$

To solve this equation, we isolate the variable (i.e., get m by itself) by multiplying both sides of the equation by 6,153 to get

$$\left(\frac{3}{7}\right) 6,153 = \left(\frac{m}{6,153}\right) 6,153 \text{ or } m = 2,637.$$

Questions

Q–69

Linda bought a jacket on sale at a 25 percent discount. If she paid $54 for the jacket, what was the original price of the jacket?

(A) $72.00 $\times .75 = 54$

(B) $67.50

(C) $54.00

(D) $40.50

Your Answer _____

Q–70

Mrs. Wall has $300,000. She wishes to give each of her six children an equal amount of her money. Which of the following methods will result in the amount that each child is to receive?

(A) $6 \times 300,000$

(B) $6 \div 300,000$

(C) $300,000 \div 6$

(D) $6 - 300,000$

Your Answer _____

325

Answers

A–69

(A)   Let p be the original price of the jacket. Linda received a 25 percent discount so she paid 75 percent of the original price. Thus, 75 percent of p equals 54. Writing this in an equation, we get

$$0.75p = 54 \text{ or } p = 54.$$

To solve this equation, multiply both sides of the equation by the reciprocal of $\frac{3}{4}$ which is $\frac{4}{3}$. This will isolate the variable p.

$$\frac{4}{3}\left(\frac{3}{4}p\right) = \left(\frac{4}{3}\right)54 \text{ or } p = \frac{216}{3} = 72$$

A–70

(C)   Another way to phrase the second sentence is: She wants to divide her money equally among her six children. Therefore, each child is to receive $300{,}000 \div 6$.

Questions

Q–71

Bob wants to bake some cupcakes. His recipe uses $2\frac{2}{3}$ cups of flour to produce 36 cupcakes. How many cups of flour should Bob use to bake 12 cupcakes?

(A) $\frac{1}{3}$

(B) $\frac{8}{9}$

(C) 1

(D) $1\frac{2}{9}$

Your Answer _____

_____

$$\frac{8}{3} = 36$$

The islets of Langerhans are the irregularly shaped patches of endocrine tissue located within the pancreas of most vertebrates. They are named for the German physician Paul Langerhans who described them in 1869. (Encyclopedia Britannica, 2017.)

Answers

A–71

(B) Bob wants to bake 12 cupcakes. The recipe is for 36 cupcakes. Therefore, Bob wants to make $^{12}/_{36}$ or $^{1}/_{3}$ of the usual amount of cupcakes. Thus, Bob should use $^{1}/_{3}$ of the recipe's flour or

$$\left(\frac{1}{3}\right)\left(\frac{8}{3}\right) = \frac{8}{9}.$$

Note we used $^{8}/_{3}$ since $^{22}/_{3} = {^{8}/_{3}}$.

Questions

Q–72

Ricky drove from Town A to Town B in 3 hours. His return trip from Town B to Town A took 5 hours because he drove 15 miles per hour slower on the return trip. How fast did Ricky drive on the trip from Town A to Town B?

(A) 25.5

(B) 32

(C) 37.5

(D) 45

Your Answer _____

_____

2 hrs more

The human growth hormone, or somatotropin, stimulates growth of essentially all tissue of the body including bone. GH is vital for normal physical growth in children. (Encyclopedia Britannica, 2017.)

Answers

A–72

(C)   Let s_1 and s_2 be Ricky's speed (rate) on the trip from A to B and the return trip from B to A, respectively. Then, since he drove 15 miles per hour slower on the return trip, $s_2 = s_1 - 15$. Recall that rate times time equals distance. So the distance from A to B is $(s_1)3 = 3s_1$ and the distance from B to A is

$$(s_2)5 = 5s_2 = 5(s_1 - 15) = 5s_1 - 75.$$

But the distance from Town A to Town B is the same as the distance from Town B to Town A, so we have the following equation:

$$3s_1 = 5s_1 - 75.$$

To solve this equation, first add 75 to both sides of the equation:

$$3s_1 + 75 = 5s_1 - 75 + 75 \text{ or } 3s_1 + 75 = 5s_1.$$

Now to isolate the variable, subtract 3s1 from both sides:

$$3s_1 + 75 - 3s_1 = 5s_1 - 3s_1 \text{ or } 75 = 2s_1.$$

To finish the problem, divide both sides of the equation by 2:

$$s_1 = \frac{75}{2} = 37.5.$$

Thus, Ricky drove 37.5 miles per hour on his trip from Town A to Town B.

Questions

Q–73

Simplify the following expression.

$$\frac{x^2 \times x^7}{x}$$

(A) x^6

(B) x^7

(C) x^8

(D) x^{10}

$\left(x\right)\left(x^6\right)$

Your Answer _____

_____

$$\left(\frac{x^2}{x}\right)\left(\frac{x^7}{x}\right) \quad x$$

$$-(-3)^2 + 2(-3)$$
$$= 9 + 6 = -15$$

Q–74

If $x = -3$, then find the value of $-x^2 + 2x$.

(A) –15

(B) –3

(C) 3

(D) 6

Your Answer _____

_____

Answers

A–73

(C) Recall the following Laws of Exponents:
$$x^p \times x^q = x^{p+q} \text{ and } \frac{x^p}{x^q} = x^{p-q}$$
So, $x^2 \times x^7 = x^{2+7} = x^9$. Hence,
$$\frac{x^2 \times x^7}{x} = \frac{x^9}{x^1} = x^{9-1} = x^8.$$

A–74

(A) If $x = -3$, then
$$-x^2 + 2x = -(-3)^2 + 2(-3) = -(9) + (-6) = -15.$$

Questions

Q–75

.125

If $a = b^3$ and $a = \frac{1}{8}$, what is the value of b?

(A) $\frac{1}{512}$

(B) $\frac{1}{8}$

(C) $\frac{3}{8}$

(D) $\frac{1}{2}$

Your Answer _____

Q–76

Solve for x in the following proportion.

$$\frac{12}{x-1} = \frac{5}{6}$$

(A) 14.6

(B) 15.4

(C) 16

(D) 16.6

$12 = \left(\frac{5}{6}\right)(x-1)$

$12 = \frac{5}{6}x - \frac{5}{6}$

$12 + \frac{5}{6} = \frac{5}{6}x$

Your Answer _____

Answers

A–75

(D) If $a = b^3$ and $a = \frac{1}{8}$, then substituting into the first equation we have

$$\frac{1}{8} = b^3 \text{ or } \left(\frac{1}{2}\right)^3 = b^3 \text{ so } b = \frac{1}{2}.$$

A–76

(B) To solve the proportion

$$\frac{12}{x-1} = \frac{5}{6}$$

multiply both sides of the equation by 6 and by ($x - 1$) so that we have

$$6(x-1) \times \frac{12}{x-1} = 6(x-1) \times \frac{5}{6} \text{ or } 72 = 5(x-1).$$

Now, use the distributive property:

$$a(b-c) = ab - ac$$

to get $72 = 5x - 5$. Add 5 to both sides of the equation: $77 = 5x$
and then divide both sides by 5:

$$x = \frac{77}{5} = 15.4$$

Questions

A hyperbola's vertices are located at $(0, -3)$ and $(0, 3)$ and its asymptote equations are $y = \pm\frac{3}{4}x$. What is an equation of the hyperbola?

(A) $9y^2 - 16x^2 = 144$

(B) $16y^2 - 9x^2 = 144$

(C) $16y^2 - 9x^2 = 1$

(D) $9y^2 - 16x^2 = 1$

Your Answer _____

_____

Answers

(B) When the vertices of a hyperbola are located on the y-axis, the general equation is given by $\dfrac{y^2}{a^2} - \dfrac{x^2}{b^2} = 1$. Then $y = \pm \dfrac{a}{b} x$ are the equations of the asymptotes. We can see that the center is at $(0, 0)$, since the asymptotes go through the center.

Since $a = 3$ and $b = 4$, we can set up the equation as $\dfrac{y^2}{3^2} - \dfrac{x^2}{4^2} = 1$, which becomes $\dfrac{y^2}{9} - \dfrac{x^2}{16} = 1$.

Multiplying by 144, we get $16y^2 - 9x^2 = 144$.

Questions

Q–78

Given the functions $f(x) = e^x - x^2$ and $g(x) = \sqrt{x-2}$, which expression below represents $g(f(2))$?

(A) 0

(B) 1

(C) $\sqrt{e^2 - 6}$

(D) -1

Your Answer _____

_____

$e^2 - 2^2$

$e^2 - 4$

$g(f(x)) \quad \sqrt{(e^x - x^2) - 2}$

$\sqrt{(e^2 - 2^2) - 2}$

$\sqrt{e^2 - 6}$

Answers

A–78

(C) $f(x) = e^x - x^2$ and $g(x) = \sqrt{x-2}$

To find $g(f(2))$, we first find $f(2)$.

Since $f(x) = e^x - x^2$, $f(2) = e^2 - 2^2 = e^2 - 4$. We now find

$$g(f(2)) = g(e^2 - 4) = \sqrt{\left(e^2 - 4\right) - 2} = \sqrt{e^2 - 6}$$

(We can verify that $\sqrt{e^2 - 6}$ is nonnegative so that $e^2 - 4$ is in the domain of $g(x)$.)

Questions

Q–79

Find an inverse function for $f(x) = \dfrac{x}{2x-1}$.

(A) $f^{-1}(x) = -\dfrac{x}{2x-1}$

(B) $f^{-1}(x) = \dfrac{x}{2x+1}$

(C) $f^{-1}(x) = \dfrac{1}{2x-1}$

(D) $f^{-1}(x) = \dfrac{x}{2x-1}$

Your Answer _____

Answers

A-79

(D) $f(x) = \dfrac{x}{2x-1}$

To form the inverse, we first write the equation as

$$y = \frac{x}{2x-1}$$

We now switch the x and y and solve for the new y.

$$x = \frac{y}{2y-1}$$

$$x(2y - 1) = y$$

$$2xy - x = y$$

$$2xy - y = x$$

$$y(2x - 1) = x$$

$$y = \frac{x}{2x-1}$$

Q–80

Which of the following is a factor of
$x^3 + 4x^2 - 23x + 6$?

(A) $(x-1)$

(B) $(x-3)$

(C) $(x+1)$

(D) $(x-2)$

$($ $)($ $)($ $)$

Your Answer _____

_____

Answers

(B) $x^3 + 4x - 23x + 6$

We can find a factor of a polynomial by several methods. One way is to take each $(x - a)$ binomial from our choices and evaluate the function at each $x = a$. If $f(a) = 0$, then $x - a$ is a factor.

We check $a = 1$ in $(x - 1)$:
$f(1) = (1)^3 + 4(1)^2 - 23(1) + 6 = -12 \neq 0$.
Therefore, $(x - 1)$ is *not* a factor.

We check $a = 3$ in $(x - 3)$:
$f(3) = (3)^3 + 4(3)^2 - 23(3) + 6 = 0$.
Therefore, $(x - 3)$ is a factor.

We check $a = -1$ in $(x + 1)$:
$f(-1) = (-1)^3 + 4(-1)^2 - 23(-1) + 6 = 32 \neq 0$.

Therefore, $(x + 1)$ is *not* a factor.

We check $a = 2$ in $(x - 2)$:
$f(2) = (2)^3 + 4(2)^2 - 23(2) + 6 = -24 \neq 0$.
Therefore, $(x - 2)$ is *not* a factor.

We check $a = -2$ in $(x + 2)$:
$f(-2) = (-2)^3 + 4(-2)^2 - 23(-2) + 6 = 60 \neq 0$.
Therefore, $(x + 2)$ is *not* a factor.

The only one of our choices that is a factor is $(x - 3)$.

Questions

If $y = 6x^2 + x$, then $\dfrac{dy}{dx} =$

(A) $12x + 1$.

(B) $12x$.

(C) $2x^3 + \dfrac{1}{2}x^2$.

(D) $13x$.

Your Answer _____

_____

A–81

(A)   Utilize the derivative formula,

$$\frac{d}{dx}\left(x^2\right) = n \cdot x^{n-1}$$

$$\frac{d}{dx}\left(6x^2 + x\right) =$$

$$(6)(2)x^{2-1} + 1x^{1-1} =$$

$$12x + 1$$

Questions

Q–82

If 406.725 is rounded off to the nearest tenth, the number is

(A) 406.3.

(B) 406.5.

(C) 406.7.

(D) 406.8.

Your Answer _____

_____

A Drug Delivery System is a means of getting medicine to the appropriate body part. These range from traditional systems such as tablets, injections, etc., to modern systems such as liposomes, transdermal patches, and those systems which are targeted to particular organs or tissues. (www.aacp.org)

Answers

A–82

(C) 7 is in the tenths place. Since the next digit (2) is below 5, drop this digit and retain the 7. The answer, therefore, is 406.7.

Questions

Q–83

The mean IQ score for 1,500 students is 100, with a standard deviation of 15. Assuming normal curve distribution, how many students have an IQ between 85 and 115? Refer to the figure shown below.

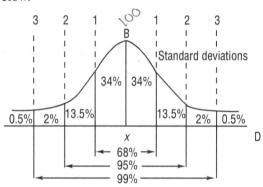

(A)   510

(B)   750

(C)   1,020

(D)   1,275

Your Answer _____

_____

Answers

A–83

(C)   The mean IQ score of 100 is given. One standard deviation above the mean is 34% of the cases, with an IQ score up to 115. One standard deviation below the mean is another 34% of the cases, with an IQ score till 85. So, a total of 68% of the students have an IQ between 85 and 115. Therefore, $1,500 \times .68 = 1,020$.

Questions

Q–84

The sum of 12 and twice a number is 24. Find the number.

(A) 6

(B) 8

(C) 10

(D) 11

Your Answer _____

$$\frac{28}{2} = 14$$

Q–85

Twice the sum of 10 and a number is 28. Find the number.

(A) 4

(B) 8

(C) 12

(D) 14

Your Answer _____

Answers

A–84

(**A**)
$$12 + 2x = 24$$
$$2x = 24 - 12$$
$$2x = 12$$
$$x = \frac{12}{2}$$
$$x = 6$$

A–85

(**A**)
$$(10 + x)2 = 28$$
$$20 + 2x = 28$$
$$2x = 28 - 20$$
$$2x = 8$$
$$x = \frac{8}{2}$$
$$x = 4$$

Questions

Two college roommates spent $2,000 for their total monthly expenses. A pie graph below indicates a record of their expenses.

2,000

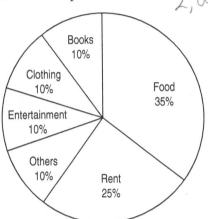

Based on the above information, which of the following statements is accurate?

(A) The roommates spent $700 on food alone.

(B) The roommates spent $550 on rent alone.

(C) The roommates spent $300 on entertainment alone.

(D) The roommates spent $300 on clothing alone.

Your Answer _____

_____

Answers

A–86

(A) $2,000 × .35 = $700.

The other answer choices have incorrect computations.

Questions

Q–87

You can buy a cell phone for $24. If you are charged $3 per month for renting a cell phone from the telephone company, how long will it take you to recover the cost of the phone if you buy one?

(A)   6 months

(B)   7 months

(C)   8 months

(D)   9 months

Your Answer _____

$$\frac{24}{3} = 8$$

Answers

A–87

(C) Let x = length of time (# of mos.) to recover cost.

$$3x = 24$$
$$x = \frac{24}{3}$$
$$x = 8 \text{ mos.}$$

Questions

Q–88

Find the value of b such that $\int_1^b 2x^{-1}\, dx = 5$.

(A) e^3

(B) $e^{2.5}$

(C) e^2

(D) 6

Your Answer _____

_____

$2\,(2.5)^{-1}$

Answers

(B) Find the value of b such that
$$\int_1^b 2x^{-1}\, dx = 5.$$

$$\int_1^b 2x^{-1}\, dx = \int_1^b \frac{2}{x}\, dx$$
$$= 2\ln(x)\big|_1^b$$
$$= 2\big[\ln(b) - \ln(1)\big]$$

$$2[\ln(b) - \ln(1)] = 5$$

$$2[\ln(b) - 0] = 5]$$

$$\ln(b) = 2.5$$

$$b = e^{2.5}$$

Questions

Q–89

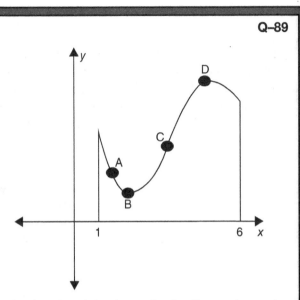

The function h is shown in the figure above. At which of the following points is h' equal to the average rate of change of h over the interval $[1, 5]$?

(A) A

(B) B

(C) C

(D) D

Your Answer _____

_____

Answers

(D) The average rate of change is the slope of a segment connecting the endpoints of the curve on the interval [1, 5]. h' is the slope of a tangent to the curve. Point D is the only given point where the slope of the tangent is equal to the slope of the segment.

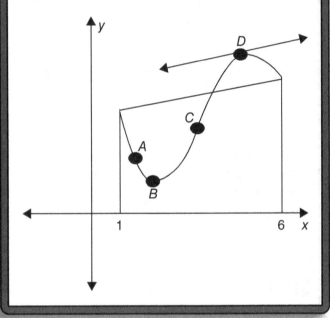

Q–90

Let g be a function defined over all real numbers and a be a constant. If $\lim\limits_{x \to a} g(x) = g(a)$, which of the following statements MUST be true?

      I. g is differentiable at $x = a$

      II. g is continuous at $x = a$

      III. g has a local minimum at $x = a$

(A) I only

(B) II only

(C) I & II only

(D) II & III only

Your Answer _____

_____

Answers

A-90

(B) $\lim_{x \to a} g(x) = g(a)$ is the necessary condition for continuity at a point, a. We know statement II is true. Differentiability at a point guarantees continuity, but continuity does not guarantee differentiability. The function g could have a cusp at $(a, g(a))$. Statement III does not have to be true since a cusp at a high point would be a local maximum, not a minimum. Only statement II must be true.

Questions

Q–91

What is $\lim\limits_{x \to 5} \dfrac{x^2 - 2x - 15}{x - 5}$?

(A) 0

(B) 1

(C) 2

(D) 8

$$\frac{5^2 - 2(5) - 15}{5 - 5}$$

Your Answer _____

_____

Answers

A-91

(D) $\lim_{x \to 5} \dfrac{x^2 - 2x - 15}{x - 5} =$

$\lim_{x \to 5} \dfrac{(x - 5)(x + 3)}{(x - 5)}$

$\lim_{x \to 5} (x + 3) = 8.$

Questions

Q–92

$$\int \tan^2 x \, dx =$$

(A) $\dfrac{\tan^3 x}{3} + C$.

(B) $\dfrac{\tan^3 x}{3\sec^2 x} + C$.

Guess

(C) $x - \tan(x) + C$.

(D) $\tan(x) - x + C$.

Your Answer _____

_____

Answers

A-92

(D)   Use a substitution from the trigonometric identity, $1 + \tan^2(x) = \sec^2 x$.

$$\int \tan^2 x \, dx = \int \left(\sec^2 x - 1 \right) dx$$
$$\int \left(\sec^2 x - 1 \right) dx = \int \sec^2 x \, dx - \int 1 \, dx$$

$$= \tan(x) - x + C$$

Questions

Q–93

Which of the following is NOT a proper subset of $\{1, 2, 3, 4\}$?

(A) $\{1, 2\}$

(B) $\{1, 2, 3\}$

(C) $\{1, 3, 4\}$

(D) $\{1, 2, 5\}$

Your Answer _____

_____

Q–94

Which of the following is an example of a rational number?

(A) $\sqrt{17}$

(B) $6\sqrt[3]{7}$

(C) $4\sqrt{11}$

(D) $7 + \sqrt{9}$

Your Answer _____

_____

Answers

A–93

(D) Only (D) has an element (which is 5) not present in the given set of {1, 2, 3, 4}.

A–94

(D) Nine is the square of an integer. 17, 11, and 15 are not squares of an integer, therefore, they are irrational numbers. 7 is not the cube of an integer; hence, it is an irrational number as well.

Questions

Which of the following statements includes a cardinal number?

(A) There are 15 volumes in the set of periodicals.

(B) I received my 14th volume recently.

(C) The students meet in Room 304.

(D) My phone number is 213-617-8442.

Your Answer _____

_____

Answers

A–95

(A) 15 is used as a cardinal number. The rest are either ordinal (B) or nominal numbers (C) and (D).

Questions

Q-96

In a group of 30 students, 12 are studying mathematics, 18 are studying English, 8 are studying science, 7 are studying both mathematics and English, 6 are studying English and science, 5 are studying mathematics and science, and 4 are studying all three subjects. How many of these students are taking only English? How many of these students are not taking any of these subjects?

(A) 9 students take only English; 6 students take none of these subjects.

(B) 10 students take only English; 5 students take none of these subjects.

(C) 11 students take only English; 5 students take none of these subjects.

(D) 12 students take only English; 6 students take none of these subjects.

Your Answer _____

3 Monly   5 Eonly   11
12M   18E   8 S = 38

7m+E   6E+S   5 m +S = 18
23   20   15 = 58

Answers

(A) Use the Venn diagram (as shown below) with three circles to represent the set of students in each of the listed subject matter areas. Start with four students taking all three subjects. We write the number 4 in the region that is the intersection of all these circles. Then we work backward: Since seven are taking math and English, and four of these have already been identified as also taking English, math, and science, there must be exactly three taking only math and English. That is, there must be three in the region representing math and English, but not science. Continuing in this manner, we enter the given data in the diagram.

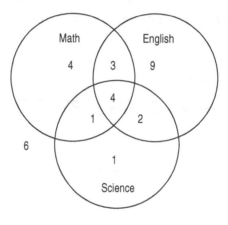

Questions

For the given Venn diagram, find n(A « B « C).

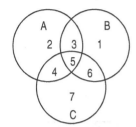

(A) 3

(B) 4

(C) 5

(D) 6

Your Answer _____

Find the next three terms in this sequence: 1, 4, 9, 16,...

(A) 19, 24, 31

(B) 20, 25, 31

(C) 21, 28, 36

(D) 25, 36, 49

Your Answer _____

Answers

A-97

(C) There is one element in the intersection of all three sets. Thus,
$$n(A \cap B \cap C) = 5.$$

A-98

(D) The sequence 1, 4, 9, 16 is the sum of the odd numbers.

1. 1
2. $1 + 3 = 4$
3. $1 + 3 + 5 = 9$
4. $1 + 3 + 5 + 7 = 16$

Questions

Q–99

Assume that one pig eats 4 pounds of food each week. There are 52 weeks in a year. How much food do 10 pigs eat in a week?

(A) 40 lb.

(B) 520 lb.

(C) 208 lb.

(D) 20 lb.

$$\left(\frac{1\,pig}{4\,lbs}\right)(52)$$

Your Answer _____

$$\begin{array}{r} 65 \\ -25 \\ \hline 40 \end{array}$$

$\dfrac{40}{2} = 20$

45

Q–100

Suppose that a pair of pants and a shirt cost $65 and the pants cost $25 more than the shirt. What did they each cost?

(A) The pants cost $35 and the shirt costs $30.

(B) The pants cost $40 and the shirt costs $25.

(C) The pants cost $43 and the shirt costs $22.

(D) The pants cost $45 and the shirt costs $20.

Your Answer _____

Answers

A–99

(A) Here one must use only the needed information. Do not be distracted by superfluous data. Simple multiplication will do. If one pig eats four pounds of food per week, how much will 10 pigs eat in one week? $10 \times 4 = 40$ pounds. The problem intentionally contains superfluous data (52 weeks), which should not distract the reader from its easy solution. Ratio and proportion will also work here

$$\frac{1}{10} = \frac{4}{x}, \; x = 40 \text{ pounds/week.}$$

A–100

(D) Let the variable S stand for the cost of the shirt. Then the cost of the pair of pants is S + 25 and

$$S + (S + 25) = 65$$
$$2S = 65 - 25$$
$$2S = 40$$
$$S = 20$$

$20 (cost of shirt)
$20 + $25 = $45 (cost of pants)

Questions

Q–101

There are five members in a basketball team. Suppose each member shakes hands with every other member of the team before the game starts; how many handshakes will there be in all?

(A) 6

(B) 8

(C) 9

(D) 10

5×5

Your Answer _____

20 10 5 2

Q–102

Tom bought a piece of land for $20,000. If he had to pay 20 percent of the price as a down payment, how much was the down payment?

(A) $2,500

(B) $3,000

(C) $4,000

(D) $4,500

Your Answer _____

Answers

A–101

(D) The possible handshakes are illustrated by listing all the possible pairs of letters, thus

AB	AC	AD	AE
BC	BD	BE	
CD	CE		
DE			

(a total of 10 handshakes)

A–102

(C) Let

$$D = \text{down payment}$$
$$D = \$20,000 \times .20$$
$$D = \$4,000$$

Questions

Q–103

A computer sells for $3,200 to the general public. If you purchase one in the university, the price is reduced by 20 percent. What is the sale price of the computer?

(A) $640

(B) $2,000

(C) $2,410

(D) $2,560

Your Answer _____

Q–104

In order for Sue to receive a final grade of C, she must have an average greater than or equal to 70% but less than 80% on five tests. Suppose her grades on the first four tests were 65%, 85%, 60%, and 90%. What range of grades on the fifth test would give her a C in the course? $65 + 85 + 60$

(A) 45 up to but excluding 95 $+ 90$

(B) 47 up to but excluding 90

(C) 49 up to but excluding 98

(D) 50 up to but excluding 100

Your Answer _____

Answers

(D)   20% of $3,200 = $640 (amount price reduced)
$3,200 − $640 = $2,560 (sale price)

A–104

(D)   Let x = 5th grade

$$\text{Average} = \frac{65 + 85 + 60 + 90 + x}{5}$$

For Sue to obtain a C, her average must be greater than or equal to 70 but less than 80.

$$70 \leq \frac{65+85+60+90+x}{5}$$

$$70 \leq \frac{300 + x < 80}{5}$$

$$5(70) \leq 5(300 + x \div 5) < 5(80)$$
$$350 \leq 300 + x < 400$$
$$350 - 300 \leq x < 400 - 300$$
$$50 \leq x < 100$$

Thus, a grade of 50 up to but not including a grade of 100 will result in a C.

Questions

Q–105

A certain company produces two types of lawn-mowers. Type A is self-propelled while type B is not. The company can produce a maximum of 18 mowers per week. It can make a profit of $15 on mower A and a profit of $20 on mower B. The company wants to make at least 2 mowers of type A but not more than 5. They also plan to make at least 2 mowers of type B. Let x be the number of type A produced, and let y be the number of type B produced.

From the above, which of the following is NOT one of the listed constraints?

(A) $x \geq 2$

(B) $x \leq 5$

(C) $x + y \leq 18$

(D) $y < 5$

Your Answer _____

_____

$x \geq 2$

$x \leq 5$

Answers

A–105

(D) The constraint for y is to at least make two mowers.

Take Quiz 3 at the REA Study Center to test your immediate grasp of the topics in this section.

(www.rea.com/studycenter)

Section IV
Critical Reading

DIRECTIONS: The following questions test your ability to interpret, analyze, and evaluate what you read.

Section IV

Critical Reading

PASSAGE 1

Types of Insulin – What is The Difference?

Lindsey Helm, PharmD

Insulin, a naturally-occurring hormone secreted by the beta cells in the pancreas,[1] allows for the cells in the body to use or store the glucose found in the blood for energy. For patients with diabetes, commercially available insulin products are a treatment option to help lower blood glucose. Currently there are more than 15 brand name formulations of insulin on the market. Among these products, there are 4 different classes of insulin. Each class is distinguished by its duration of action or how long the insulin continues to lower blood glucose (eg, rapid-, short-, intermediate-, and long-acting); this impacts how the patient will use the product to control their blood glucose. Additionally, insulin products differ by cost, route of administration, and formulation.

Diabetes was first recognized by the ancient Egyptians around 1500 B.C. Before the invention of exogenous insulin in the 1920s, diabetes was recognized to be fatal within weeks to months after diagnosis[2]; however, this is not the case today. It is estimated that 21 million Americans are currently diagnosed with diabetes. Of those, an estimated 28.7% report using a commercially available insulin product to manage their diabetes.[3]

A common chronic disease, diabetes causes blood glucose levels to be higher than normal due to defects in insulin secretion, insulin action, or both.[4] The chronic high blood glucose of diabetes is associated with long-term damage, dysfunction, and failure of various organs in the body, especially the eyes, kidneys, nerves, heart, and blood vessels. People with a genetic predisposition, who are physically inactive, have hypertension, a low HDL cholesterol level (35 mg/dL [0.90 mmol/L] or less) and/or a high triglyceride level (250 mg/dL or more), a history of cardiovascular disease (CVD), and/or are obese (body mass index [BMI] 27.5 kg/m^2 or greater) have the highest risk of developing diabetes.[5] According to the CDC, there are about 8.1 million Americans who are currently undiagnosed with diabetes.[3]

For the majority of patients, diabetes can generally be classified as either type 1 or type 2.[1] Because it helps regulate metabolism (the chemical processes necessary to maintain life), insulin can be used for either type. Insulin is classified as a hormone, and its chemical structure is composed of amino acids, which makes it a protein. Insulin binds to insulin receptors on cells throughout the body.[4] Once the insulin binds to the receptors, it helps the cells move glucose out of the blood and into the cell, where glucose is used as energy to carry out normal cellular functions. In a normal functioning pancreas, insulin is secreted by the beta cells in small amounts throughout the day without regard to meals; this is referred to as basal secretion. When a meal or snack is ingested, the pancreas increases production of insulin in response to the increased levels of blood glucose from the digestion of food.[5] This type of insulin release is referred to as prandial secretion.

Refer to the above passage for questions 1 – 10.

Questions

Q–1

What is the main idea of the passage?

(A) Diabetes was first recognized by ancient Egyptians.

(B) Diabetes is managed using commercially available insulin products.

(C) Identify insulin's role in managing diabetes.

(D) Diabetes is associated with long-term organ damage.

Your Answer _____

_____

Q–2

What is the author's purpose for writing this passage?

(A) Tell the reader anecdotal facts about diabetes.

(B) Inform the reader about diabetes and the use of insulin.

(C) Persuade the reader that insulin is the best treatment available.

(D) Sway the reader into believing that diabetes is not curable.

Your Answer _____

_____

Answers

A–1

(C)   Rationale: The main idea of a passage can often be found in the introduction or conclusion. Also, check the beginning, middle, and end of a paragraph. Although all the statements listed are true, only option C presents the main idea of the passage.

A–2

(B)   Rationale: The author's purpose is supposed to be deduced by the reader upon reading the passage. The passage is very scientific. It is not introducing any anecdotal facts. It also does not have a persuading or swaying tone.

Questions

Q–3

Which of the following is implied by the passage?

(A) Diabetes is fatal.

(B) Diabetes should be managed because high blood glucose levels can lead to long-term damage to various organs.

(C) Diabetes is reversible.

(D) Insulin raises the blood glucose levels.

Your Answer _____

_____

Q–4

What can be inferred from the second paragraph?

(A) Diabetes can be managed with the use of insulin.

(B) Diabetes is a common chronic disease.

(C) Diabetes is almost always fatal.

(D) A large amount of Americans are diagnosed with diabetes every year.

Your Answer _____

_____

Answers

A–3

(B) Rationale: To imply is to suggest something indirectly. All of the other statements are incorrect.

A–4

(A) Rationale: To infer is to conclude based on stated facts. The second paragraph is focusing on the management of diabetes with insulin.

Questions

Q–5

According to the last sentence in the 4th paragraph, which of the following is a definition of prandial?

(A) Increase in production of insulin

(B) Ingestion of a meal or snack

(C) Relating to food digestion

(D) Increased levels of blood glucose

Your Answer _____

_____

Q–6

Which of the following words best describes the author's tone?

(A) Opinionated

(B) Facetious

(C) Forceful

(D) Explanatory

Your Answer _____

_____

Answers

A–5

(C) Rationale: Look for the synonym that makes the most sense based on the context. All of the other options are not correct definitions.

A–6

(D) Rationale: The tone is explanatory because the author is only stating facts rather than opinions, suggestions, or analysis. The author's tone does not sound opinionated, facetious, or forceful.

Questions

Q-7

Choose the best summary of the passage.

(A) Insulin is a naturally occurring hormone secreted by the pancreas.

(B) Diabetes can generally be classified as either Type 1 or Type 2.

(C) There are currently about 8.1 million Americans who have undiagnosed diabetes.

(D) Insulin is a treatment option for diabetes and can help manage blood glucose levels.

Your Answer _____

_____

Q-8

Who is the intended audience?

(A) Healthcare professionals

(B) The general public

(C) Consumers

(D) Stakeholders

Your Answer _____

_____

Answers

A-7

(D) Rationale: The summary should reiterate the main idea of the passage. Although the other statements are true, they do not summarize the main idea of the passage.

A-8

(A) Rationale: The target audience is the intended group of people that the author is trying to reach with his writing. This article is geared towards healthcare professionals.

Questions

Q-9

Which of the following is the best possible title for the passage?

(A) The Chronic High Blood Glucose of Diabetes

(B) What is Diabetes?

(C) Diabetes Management in America

(D) Diabetes Health Management with Insulin

Your Answer _____

_____

Q-10

Which of the following can be inferred from the last sentence in the 3rd paragraph?

(A) Diabetes is a major problem in America.

(B) A large segment of the American population is living with diabetes and don't know they have the disease.

(C) Insulin is a treatment option for diabetes and can help manage blood glucose levels.

(D) The CDC recommends better diagnosis of diabetes.

Your Answer _____

_____

Answers

(D) Rationale: A title summarizes the main idea of the passage and prepares the reader for the type of information presented in the body of the passage. The content is mainly focused on management of diabetes using insulin.

(B) Rationale: To infer is to conclude based on stated facts. The last sentence suggests that a lot of people are living with diabetes but are unaware of the disease.

PASSAGE 2
Strategic Thinking in Pharmacy

Anthony M. Boyd, John S. Clark and
Stan S. Kent

Healthcare within the United States is undergoing a major transformation. Health-system leaders are under immense pressure to ensure the quality of care while maximizing value for patients.[1] Likewise, the profession of pharmacy is changing due to a number of factors: exponentially rising drug costs, the shift from inpatient to outpatient care, risk- and value-based reimbursement, the use of digital health technology, and the potential use of "big data" to guide treatment decisions. It is imperative for pharmacy leaders to begin to think strategically and become visionaries to remain relevant in the future of healthcare.

There is a common misconception that strategic thinking and strategic planning are the same. Executives can limit the breadth of their strategic thinking efforts by overlapping the two ideas. Strategic thinking is completed at random through multiple channels and results in the creation of a vision through innovation. Strategic planning is a method of implementing existing strategies on a scheduled timeline through the use of organizational tools by using ideas created during the strategic-thinking process.[2] Pharmacy leaders often further narrow their scope to operational planning, which emphasizes day-to-day planning that allows the department to function. Pharmacists' clinical services are a direct result of innovation. The doctor of pharmacy degree and completion of residency training are examples of results of strategic thinking: imagining what could be and then putting plans in place to achieve that vision. Pharmacy leaders must look beyond what has previously been done, find creative solutions to healthcare challenges, and embrace these changes to move the profession forward. Strategic leaders need to imagine what *could* be.

Although strategic thinking has been well described in other areas of business and healthcare, pharmacy-specific literature is focused on strategic planning.[3–6] Through the establishment of the pharmacy enterprise, pharmacy leaders assume responsibility for the entire medication-use continuum within a health system, with specific emphasis on patient outcomes, quality, and financial success.[7] According to Weber,[6] strategic planning is composed of the following: analysis, use of planning groups, and execution. Given the lack of pharmacy literature with regard to strategic thinking, we have written this article in hopes of providing insight and motivation for pharmacy leaders to influence the practice of pharmacy in the coming years.

(Originally published in July 2017, Copyright © American Society of Health-System Pharmacists, Inc. All rights reserved. Reprinted with permission.)

Refer to the above passage for questions 11 – 18.

Questions

Q–11

Which of the following words best describes the author's tone?

(A) Opinionated

(B) Facetious

(C) Forceful

(D) Explanatory

Your Answer _____

_____

Answers

A–11

(A)   Rationale: This passage is presenting the author's opinion on strategic thinking. The author's tone is not facetious, forceful, or explanatory.

Questions

Q–12

Which of the following sentences is an opinion?

(A) Pharmacy leaders must look beyond what has previously been done, find creative solutions to healthcare challenges, and embrace these changes to move the profession forward.

(B) According to Weber, strategic planning is composed of the following: analysis, use of planning groups, and execution.

(C) Strategic thinking is completed at random through multiple channels and results in the creation of a vision through innovation.

(D) Pharmacy leaders assume responsibility for the entire medication-use continuum within a health system, with specific emphasis on patient outcomes, quality, and financial success.

Your Answer _____

_____

Answers

A–12

(A)   Rationale: The author is clearly stating his opinion whereas the other sentences are introducing facts based on supportive evidence.

Questions

Q–13

Who is the intended audience?

(A) Pharmacy leaders

(B) The general public

(C) Consumers

(D) Stakeholders

Your Answer _____

_____

Q–14

What is the author's purpose for writing this passage?

(A) To criticize pharmacy professionals

(B) To provide insight to influence the practice of pharmacy

(C) To inform the public about common misconceptions surrounding strategic thinking

(D) To discuss changes in the pharmacy profession

Your Answer _____

_____

Answers

A–13

(A) Rationale: The target audience is the intended group of people that the author is trying to reach with his writing. This passage is aimed at pharmacy leaders.

A–14

(B) Rationale: The author's purpose is supposed to be deduced by the reader upon reading the passage. The author is interested in influencing the practice of pharmacy.

Questions

Q–15

What is the main idea of the passage?

(A) Drug costs are rising.

(B) Pharmacists' clinical services are a direct result of innovation.

(C) Pharmacy leaders need to think strategically to remain relevant in the future of healthcare.

(D) Pharmacy-specific literature is focused on strategic planning.

Your Answer _____

_____

Q–16

What is one of the concerns raised by the passage?

(A) It is important for pharmacy leaders to become visionaries.

(B) Innovation is important in pharmacy.

(C) Operational planning is key.

(D) There is a lack of pharmacy literature on strategic planning.

Your Answer _____

_____

Answers

A–15

(C) Rationale: The main idea of a passage can often be found in the introduction or conclusion. Also, check the beginning, middle, and end of a paragraph. Although the other statements are true, only choice (C) presents the main idea of the passage.

A–16

(A) Rationale: Although innovation is important in pharmacy, this is not stated anywhere in the passage. The only concern raised by the passage is listed in choice (A.) The rest of the statements do not introduce any concerns. Choice (D) is an incorrect statement because according to the author, there is a lack of pharmacy literature on strategic thinking and not on planning.

Q–17

Which of the following statements can be deduced from the article?

(A) Strategic thinking cannot be achieved without strategic planning.

(B) Strategic thinking involves analysis, planning groups, and execution.

(C) Strategic planning requires that pharmacy leaders become visionaries.

(D) Strategic thinking encourages pharmacy leaders to find creative solutions.

Your Answer _____

_____

Answers

A–17

(D) Rationale: The first statement is incorrect. Strategic planning would actually depend on strategic thinking. Option (B) is true of strategic planning. Option (C) is true of strategic thinking. Option (D) presents the only correct statement.

Questions

Q–18

Which of the following statements is made by the author to support his claim: "Healthcare within the United States is undergoing a major transformation"?

(A) Drug costs are rising exponentially.

(B) Pharmacy leaders lack innovation.

(C) Maximizing value to patients while ensuring the quality of care is emphasized more than ever.

(D) Health system leaders are under pressure to improve the quality of care.

Your Answer _____

_____

Answers

A–18

(C)   Rationale: Option (A) is a correct statement. However, it is not used as a supporting fact for the opening statement. Option (B) is an anecdotal statement that can be deduced from the article. Option (D) is correct. However, the author doesn't use the need for improving care as a supporting fact for his opening statement. Option (C) states the supporting fact used by the author for his opening statement.

PASSAGE 3
Drug Shortage: Unexpected Reward

Jeannette Y. Wick, RPh, MBA, FASCP

Serendipity and medicine is a wonderful thing. It was serendipity that allowed Fleming to discover penicillin in the 1940s, and serendipity that led Von Mering and Minkowski to determine that diabetes was a disease of the pancreas.

Serendipity and pharmacy practice is the topic of an article published in *BMG Quality & Safety*. Written by a team of pharmacists from the University of Texas Southwestern Medical Center in Dallas, Texas, it describes how a drug shortage led to the adoption of a high-value care practice.

According to the authors, prescribers often view change introduced to save money as suspicious regardless of whether they are evidence-based and will have no adverse effect on quality of care. These pharmacists had faced resistance to limiting the number of proton pump inhibitors (PPIs), and particularly, use of oral drugs as opposed to intravenous drugs under appropriate circumstances.

It was a shortage of a specific intravenous PPI and a price increase of 344% that stimulated change. This dilemma prompted the pharmacists to perform retrospective review for all intravenous PPIs in the year preceding the shortage. They found that the average cost per month for intravenous PPIs approach $12,000, and most of the orders came from wards (as opposed to intensive care units, postoperative care units, or the emergency department).

Clearly, any change they could implement would be "high-value."

Due to a pressing need to address intravenous PPIs, they implemented (and prescribers rapidly adopted) interventions that led to a 76% decrease in intravenous PPI use. After the drug shortage resolved, they continued the identical interventions, and sustained the decrease. They estimate that the cumulative savings are roughly $200,000.

More importantly, prescribing practices changed. Prescribers were more likely to use prebuilt order sets and, pharmacists were less likely to have to intervene.

The authors also discussed concerns of purchasing drugs that are in shortage status from secondary sources. They concluded that colleagues need to work diligently to lower health care costs without sacrificing quality to increase value.

Refer to the above passage for questions 19 – 21.

Questions

Q–19

What is the tone of the author?

(A) Ironic

(B) Cynical

(C) Depressed

(D) Positive

Your Answer _____

_____

Q–20

How did the author team from TSMC support their argument that "prescribers often view change introduced to save money as suspicious"?

(A) Pharmacists faced resistance to use of oral drugs as opposed to intravenous drugs when appropriate.

(B) Prescribers prefer intravenous drugs for their patients.

(C) Intravenous drugs work better than oral medications.

(D) Oral drugs are more cost effective.

Your Answer _____

_____

Answers

A–19

(D) Rationale: The opening paragraph shows that the author is positive about the article she is summarizing. Her tone is not ironic, cynical, or depressed.

A–20

(A) Rationale: The statement made in option (B) is not stated anywhere in the passage. The statement in option (C) is also a claim that is not discussed in the passage. Even if option (D) is a correct statement, it is not used by the team as supportive evidence.

Questions

Q–21

Who is the intended audience?

(A) Healthcare workers

(B) The general public

(C) Pharmacy professionals

(D) Authors

Your Answer _____

_____

Answers

A–21

(C) Rationale: Pharmacy professionals are the intended audience as evidenced by the following statement in the last paragraph: "…colleagues need to work diligently to lower health care costs without sacrificing quality to increase value."

PASSAGE 4

Be the Change You Wish to See In Pharmacy

Adam Martin, PharmD, ACSM-CPT

I love where I went to school! Not because of the sports teams or the parties, but because of the quality of education and superb support system that the school offers their students.

Now, there are many pharmacy schools across the United States, and many of them are good, but for me the University of Pittsburgh School of Pharmacy is unmatched in the complete quality of education that they offer to their student body. The curriculum is well organized, diverse, and paired with a solid support system of both faculty and pharmacy students; it is CLEAR that the goal is for you to learn, succeed, and grow as a leader in the pharmacy profession.

I could write a book about why the school is so unique in helping students succeed in developing leadership qualities that business owners and corporations dream about hiring, but even that would not do a justice to the school. Regardless, that is not the focus of this article; recognizing where you came from, and all the people in your life that helped you to get where you are today, should lead you to a question that I would like help in answering: how can I do the same? How can I help those who are starting from day one on a career path similar to mine? The answer, I say, is simple: give back.

Money, of course, is your first intuitive realization but I would argue that there are much more MEANINGFUL ways to give back and make a lasting impression and a difference to help others advance in their endeavors.

Mentorship is something I would define as priceless to someone pursuing a career. It provides guidance, confidence, and a 2-way learning relationship. Yes, the teacher DOES become the student! You took the path that student is now taking. You experienced the difficulties, the setbacks, the joys, and epiphanies along the way, so why not share those with someone just starting out? Yes, everyone has different experiences, and yes, not everyone has EXACTLY the same targeted career destination, but words of wisdom and experiences can prove *invaluable*.

I have always enjoyed organizing and planning projects and events (yes, I may be crazy but I love it!) ever since I became an Eagle Scout at the age of 14. Once I decided I wanted to become a pharmacist, I joined a pharmacy organization that paired pre-pharmacy students with students enrolled in the school of pharmacy to offer mentorship in assisting aspiring undergraduates to successfully meet the requirements for earning admittance into the school of pharmacy.

While attending the meetings, I noticed how good the president was at conducting the meetings, delivering information, and communicating with his co-chairs, so I took the initiative to introduce myself, and soon enough he became my mentor and good friend, still to this day.

When I was a student in pharmacy school, I started to realize that I really loved teaching (I still do, now even more so!), so I approached my favorite teacher in pharmacy school and formed a mentorship so that she could impart all her years of wisdom and experiences in how I could best develop my teaching abilities.

I tell you these stories to offer advice from my own experiences, to hopefully help you in your own endeavors:

1. Take the initiative. Don't just go through the motions and follow the syllabus! Yes, grades are important, but what you do outside of the classroom has more pull in your future than you'd think.

2. Don't be afraid. Nothing good is easy, and there are no free lunches (except for the samples at Costco). So step up! The only thing holding you back is you. Take that leap and reap the rewards!

3. Do it NOW. If you don't seize the opportunity, someone else will. Then you will apply for a job and guess what—there's only one job opening, and guess who the other person applying will be?

If you have reached a point in your career where you believe you have something valuable that students could learn from, I BEG YOU to please give back. It is likely that someone once gave *you* that privilege and took you under their wing, so return the favor to the future generations! Perhaps you were not so lucky and did not have anyone to offer you guidance—why not change the precedent, and pay it forward?

Make a difference in someone's life! Be the change you wish to see in the world! And lead by *example*—others will follow by your footsteps, so leave a legacy and lasting change for the better.

Refer to the above passage for questions 22 – 24.

Questions

Q–22

What is the tone of the author?

(A) Sadistic

(B) Depressed

(C) Enthusiastic

(D) Negative

Your Answer _____

Q–23

Who is the intended audience?

(A) Healthcare workers

(B) Pharmacy students

(C) The general public

(D) Pharmacists

Your Answer _____

Answers

A-22

(C)   Rationale: The author's tone is very enthusiastic. The tone is not sadistic, depressed, or negative. Choices (A), (B), and (D) could have been easily eliminated because they all have negative connotations.

A-23

(B)   Rationale: Pharmacy students are the target audience. The author is speaking to pharmacy students and future pharmacists.

Q–24

What is the author's purpose for writing this passage?

(A) The author is shedding light on why pharmacy school is so unique in helping students succeed in developing leadership qualities that business owners and corporations dream about.

(B) The author is sharing his experience in pharmacy school.

(C) The author is giving advice to pharmacy students based on his own experience.

(D) The author is encouraging pharmacy professionals to give back.

Your Answer _____

_____

Answers

A–24

(C) Rationale: Option (C) is the best answer in terms of its alignment with the author's purpose for writing the passage. The other statements do not introduce the author's purpose.

PASSAGE 5
Zora Neale Hurston
(1891–1960)

Jacob Stratman, Ph.D.

A key and controversial figure of the Harlem Renaissance, Zora Neale Hurston lived a life as complex and tragic as her characters. She was educated at Howard University and Barnard College where she began a career as a writer and an anthropologist. Under the direction of Franz Boas, Hurston studied black southern culture as it pertained to speech, dance, art, religion, and folklore in her hometown of Eatonville, Florida (one of the first intentional all-black communities). This study produced a highly successful book, *Mules and Men* (1935), that helped earn her a Guggenheim Fellowship to continue anthropological work. However, a year earlier, Hurston had published her first novel, *Jonah's Gourd Vine*, and it was such a literary work that it garnered the most attention from her fellow Harlem writers. Hurston did not believe that black writers should write to white audiences, yet her contemporaries like Richard Wright and Langston Hughes accused her of pandering to whites' stereotypes of blacks. Drawing upon her knowledge of black southern culture, Hurston created complex and complicated characters, and she used dialect and colloquial speech in books that contained raw discussions of the black experience. Sadly, though, Hurston wrote several more books that were rejected by publishers, and she moved back to Florida where she worked as a maid. She died destitute and forgotten in 1960 in a welfare home; her body was buried in an unmarked grave. Some historians argue that if it were not for author Alice Walker, who helped revitalize interest in her work, Hurston might still be a forgotten literary figure.

Hurston's most acclaimed work, *Their Eyes Were Watching God* (1937), is one of the most important and controversial novels of the Harlem Renaissance. The story of Janie Crawford and her return to

Eatonville, Fla., the novel explores themes that include gender, sexuality and self-identity as well as race. An author who died in near obscurity, Hurston is now recognized as an uncompromising and inspirational figure in American literature.

Refer to the above passage for questions 25 – 31.

Questions

Q–25

What is the tone of the author?

(A) Didactic

(B) Sympathetic

(C) Solemn

(D) Sarcastic

Your Answer _____

_____

Q–26

Who is the intended audience?

(A) Healthcare workers

(B) The general public

(C) Instructors

(D) Authors

Your Answer _____

_____

Answers

A–25

(A) Rationale: Didactic because the author attempts to educate the reader about the story of Hurston. There is some sympathy in the passage, but the overall theme is to educate the audience. The author's tone is neither sympathetic nor sarcastic.

A–26

(B) Rationale: The author is not speaking to one specific audience. Instead, his tone is very broad and encompassing.

Questions

Q–27

Which of the following most closely matches the meaning of the word *pandering* used in the following sentence? "Hurston did not believe that black writers should write to white audiences, yet her contemporaries like Richard Wright and Langston Hughes accused her of pandering to whites' stereotypes of blacks."

(A) Procuring

(B) Embracing

(C) Appeasing

(D) Dismissing

Your Answer _____

_____

Answers

A–27

(C)   Rationale: *Pandering* in this sentence suggests that the author is appeasing white readers' stereotypes of blacks. The other answers do not have that meaning because to pander means to do everything another person (or group) wishes.

Questions

How did the author support his claim that "Zora Neale Hurston lived a life as complex and tragic as her characters"?

(A) She was raised in an all-black community yet she appeased white audiences.

(B) Her first novel garnered the most attention from her fellow Harlem writers.

(C) Hurston created complex and complicated characters, and she used dialect and colloquial speech in books that contained raw discussions of the black experience.

(D) She was a notable writer and an anthropologist, yet she worked as a maid and died destitute and forgotten.

Your Answer _____

_____

Answers

A–28

D   Although options (A), (B), and (C) present accurate statements, only option (D) shows tragedy in the life of the author.

Q–29

What is the author's purpose for writing this passage?

(A) The author is shedding light on the life of a person who is important in American literature but whose literary work almost went unnoticed.

(B) The author is introducing the fact that Harlem writers did not like white audiences.

(C) The author is highlighting the fact that if it were not for author Alice Walker, Hurston might still be a forgotten literary figure.

(D) The author is introducing the fact that Hurston, who is recognized as an inspirational figure in American literature, worked as a maid.

Your Answer _____

_____

Answers

A-29

(A) Rationale: The statement in option (B) is not mentioned anywhere in the article. Although options (C) and (D) are correct statements, they do not present the author's purpose for writing this passage.

Questions

Q–30

The author would most likely agree with which of the following statements?

(A) Author Alice Walker contributed to the popularity of Hurston during the Harlem Renaissance.

(B) Hurston's most acclaimed work is one of the most controversial novels in history.

(C) Author Alice Walker revived interest in the work of Hurston.

(D) Hurston's most acclaimed work garnered the most attention from her fellow Harlem writers.

Your Answer _____

_____

Q–31

What is the best possible title for the passage?

(A) The Tragic Life of Zora Neale Hurston

(B) A Forgotten Prodigy

(C) The Writers of the Harlem Renaissance

(D) Important and Controversial Authors

Your Answer _____

_____

Answers

A–30

(C) Rationale: Author Alice Walker revived interest in the work of Hurston. However, she did not contribute to her popularity during the Harlem Renaissance. Although, Hurston's most acclaimed work is controversial, it is not the most controversial in history. Also, Hurston's first novel garnered the most attention from her fellow Harlem writers rather than her most acclaimed work.

A–31

(A) Rationale: The passage focuses on the tragic life of Zora Neale Hurston rather than the writers of the Harlem Renaissance or important and controversial authors. The passage does not describe Hurston as a prodigy; however, it does characterize her as an almost forgotten and important author.

PASSAGE 6
Lyndon Johnson's Great Society

Lynn Marlowe, M.A.

Lyndon Johnson's "Great Society" was the collective name for several separate programs aimed at ending civil rights abuses and combating poverty. In the area of civil rights, the Civil Rights Act of 1964 was a piece of landmark legislation. It forbade discrimination based on race, color, religion, sex, or national origin in job hiring, promotion, and firing. It also forbade such discrimination in access to public accommodations and gave the federal government powers to cut funding to federally aided industries or agencies found guilty of discrimination. It also actively involved the United States government in attacking segregated school systems and forcing them to desegregate.

Related to this, the Voting Rights Act of 1965 gave the government the power to intervene and supervise voter registration in areas where minorities had been illegally restricted or discouraged from registering to vote in significant numbers. Economically, Johnson declared a war on poverty, backing several bills to combat poverty and its causes in the United States. Medicare, followed by Medicaid, was aimed at providing quality medical care to the elderly. Several programs were initiated to increase the quality of teachers and education in poverty-stricken areas. Most notably, Project Head Start, which attempted to provide quality pre-school training for impoverished pre-schoolers, involved the government in attacking the failure to succeed in school, which marked the lives of so many of the nation's poor.

Johnson also initiated the Neighborhood Youth Corps and the Job Corps to provide job training and experience for inner city youths. There were also tax cuts and economic aid programs to provide increased welfare benefits, especially to mothers with young children. While the programs showed some initial success, and some programs such as Project Head Start were undeniably successful, many of the programs were tied to qualifications that helped lead to the destruction of the family unit among those seeking aid. Some economists argue that there is more poverty now than there was before the "Great Society" programs began. Many programs led to long-term dependence on government aid rather than fostering the independence needed to get off government support. While the civil rights aspects of the "Great Society" were quite successful in ending legal abuses to civil rights, many abuses continue today, albeit at a more subtle, insidious level. So, while the intentions of Johnson's "Great Society" programs were clearly good, the results were a mixed success.

Refer to the above passage for questions 32 – 38.

Questions

Q–32

What is the tone of the author?

(A) Condemning

(B) Enthusiastic

(C) Narrative

(D) Solemn

Your Answer _____

Q–33

Which of the following laws ended segregation of the school systems?

(A) The Civil Rights Act of 1964

(B) The Voting Rights Act of 1965

(C) The Smoot-Hawley Tariffs

(D) Project Head Start

Your Answer _____

Answers

A–32

(C) Rationale: The author's tone is narrative. The author is not condemning, enthusiastic, or solemn.

A–33

(A) Rationale: The Civil Rights Act of 1964 forced school systems to desegregate. The Voting Rights Act, the Smoot-Hawley Tariffs, and Project Head Start did not have anything to do with segregation.

Questions

What is the author's purpose for writing this passage?

(A)   To evaluate Lyndon Johnson's Great Society

(B)   To describe Lyndon Johnson's Great Society

(C)   To persuade the reader regarding the good in Lyndon Johnson's Great Society

(D)   To express concern regarding the horrific outcome of Lyndon Johnson's Great Society

Your Answer _____

_____

Answers

A–34

(B)   Rationale: The author is not evaluating, rather he is educating the reader regarding the historical events that shaped our current society. Also, the author is not persuading the reader or expressing any concerns.

Questions

What does the author use to support his argument that the results of Johnson's Great Society programs were mixed although his intentions were good?

(A) The United States government was involved in attacking segregated school systems and forcing them to desegregate.

(B) They allowed racist governments in the South to set up "separate but unequal" facilities.

(C) The programs led to long-term dependence on government aid.

(D) Many civil rights abuses continued even though the civil rights aspects were successful.

Your Answer _____

_____

Answers

(D) Rationale: Only option (D) shows the mixed results of Johnson's Great Society programs. The other options present correct statements but they do not accurately answer this question.

Q–36

What assumptions or biases are hidden within this passage?

(A) The Voting Rights Act of 1965 gave the government the power to intervene and supervise voter registration in areas where minorities had been illegally restricted from voting.

(B) Many programs led to long-term dependence on government aid rather than fostering the independence needed to get off government support.

(C) The U.S. Supreme Court struck down desegregation laws and upheld the doctrine of segregated "separate but equal" facilities for blacks and whites.

(D) The Civil Rights Act forbade discrimination based on race, color, religion, sex, or national origin in job hiring, promotion, and firing.

Your Answer _____

_____

Answers

(B)   Rationale: Only option (B) is a matter of opinion and it could be a controversial statement. All the other options are stating facts.

Questions

Q–37

Which of the following is a possible title for the passage?

(A) Voting Rights

(B) The End to Segregation

(C) The Great Society Programs

(D) A Flopped Plan

Your Answer _____

_____

Q–38

The author would most likely agree with which statement?

(A) If you don't seize opportunities, you will miss out.

(B) People should be careful about taking chances.

(C) Grades are the most important in determining one's future.

(D) Mentorship is a good option for someone pursuing a career.

Your Answer _____

_____

Answers

A–37

(C) Rationale: The article focuses on introducing the Great Society programs and history surrounding them. Voting rights and segregation are mentioned briefly as part of cause-effect of the Great Society programs.

A–38

(A) Rationale: The author believes in taking leaps of faith and seizing opportunities whenever present as to not miss out. He also states that grades are important but not the most important in determining one's future. Though a good option, mentorship is not mentioned in this passage.

PASSAGE 7
Becoming an Empathetic Reader
DAWN HOGUE, M.A.

Empathy is the ability to put yourself in someone else's place, to see things as he or she sees them. As readers, we must be empathetic if we are to truly understand the books we read. To do this means to actually put yourself in the place of the speaker, the narrator or the character.

When you read, visualize yourself in the text. Make a little mind movie in which you walk through the setting, follow the characters, listen to them speak, and observe their actions. Allow yourself to see and hear what the speaker sees and hears. Even more importantly, allow yourself to feel what the speaker feels. This is empathy.

To be fair, it is much easier to empathize with the action of fictional characters in narratives. They are like us in a direct way. But quite often instead you will need to read nonfiction prose, such as essays, diaries, memoirs, even letters. Such works typically feature one speaker writing about one topic. However, if you can't identify with this voice, you will have a difficult time discerning the main point of the essay. Even a purely expository essay will have some recognizable elements that help us visualize the text: setting (context of time and space), character (the speaker and any others necessary to the text), conflict (a problem to solve, an issue that begs exploration), even imagery (look for what you can perceive with your senses to help you fully experience the text).

At times, it will be very necessary for you to determine the attitude or identify the point of view of a speaker. If you can become an empathetic reader, this task will be much easier for you.

The more you practice empathetic reading, the more you will develop a kind of "double vision," where you'll view the text from within and also from without as a critical reader who sees the parts as they relate to the whole.

In your double vision, you'll learn to appreciate how the writing conveys enduring or short-lived and universal or disturbing ideas through the perspective of a character, narrator, or speaker.

Refer to the above passage for questions 39 – 42.

Questions

Q–39

In paragraph 3, what is the meaning of the word *expository*?

(A) Explanation

(B) Exposition

(C) Deposit

(D) Digression

Your Answer _____

Q–40

What is the author's purpose for writing the passage?

(A) To make people feel better

(B) To aid readers to gain more insight into a passage

(C) To show how difficult it is to be an empathetic reader

(D) To show you can't develop empathy with nonfiction prose

Your Answer _____

Answers

A–39

(A)   In this setting, since the author uses the word "simply," the writer means a work that merely explains a piece of information. The other three choices do not mean *explain*.

A–40

(B)   The author gives various specific suggestions to help the reader practice empathetic reading. These include using a "mind movie" to walk through the setting, follow the characters, listen to them speak, and observe their actions. She also emphasizes the importance of identifying with the writer. The notions of "feeling" (A) or failure ((C) and (D)) do not appear in the passage.

Q-41

What is the author's tone in the passage?

(A) Flippant

(B) Discriminatory

(C) Enthusiastic

(D) Downbeat

Your Answer _____

_____

Q-42

The author supports her premise that becoming an empathetic reader can be achieved by citing several recognizable elements such as

(A) visualizing outer space.

(B) visualizing the setting.

(C) reading diaries.

(D) problem solving.

Your Answer _____

_____

Answers

A–41

(C) The author's tone is that of encouragement and enthusiasm. She offers a variety of skills to the reader, fully confident that if these ideas are followed, the reader will appreciate what a piece of writing conveys. There is little negative tone in the passage.

A–42

(B) The author, in paragraph 2, states that visualizing the setting of a piece (context of time and space), helps a reader to more clearly discern the article. Though she mentions space, the author does not advise traveling to space, nor does she include reading diaries and problem solving as specific ways to become an empathetic reader.

PASSAGE 8

The Demise of the Plains Indians

ADAPTED FROM: LYNN MARLOWE, M.A.

The Plains Indians depended upon buffalo for almost every aspect of their survival. When they killed a buffalo, they used virtually every part of it: eating the meat and using its hide for clothing and shelter. They used the sinews as bowstrings, and the strong bones as tools and weapons. Buffalo fat was used as grease to water-proof containers, the hoofs used to make glue, and even buffalo dung was used for campfires. In 1850, over 13 million buffalo meandered along the migration routes in the Great Plains.

Between 1872 and 1875, only three years, white hunters killed 9 million buffalo, most often taking the skin and leaving the carcass to rot in waste. By 1890, fewer than 1,000 remained. Without the buffalo, the Plains Indians could not live according to their traditional ways. They were forced to either adapt to white rules (usually on reservations) or fight for their survival, as the Sioux and Cheyenne did in the 1870s. Fighting the whites was hopeless, but to many Indians, war was more honorable than dying in subjugation. While they managed a few victories such as at Little Big Horn, they were too badly outmanned and outgunned to have a long-term chance at victory. Without the buffalo, the entire Indian way of life was undermined and it led directly to the destruction of the Plains Indians' societies.

Refer to the above passage for questions 43 – 46.

Questions

Q–43

What does the author contend was the most important factor in the destruction of the Plains Indians' societies by whites in the late 1800s?

(A) The use of modern guns by white cavalrymen

(B) The destruction of the buffalo herds

(C) The introduction of alcohol by whites into Indian society

(D) The use of reservations by whites to limit the movement of Indians

Your Answer _____

_____

Q–44

What is the main idea of the passage?

(A) In 1875, there were 9 million free-ranging buffalo on the plains.

(B) The way of life of the plains Indians was destroyed with the slaughter of the buffalo herds.

(C) The Sioux and Cheyenne went peacefully to the reservations.

(D) The Indian victory at Little Big Horn allowed the Native American peoples to live in peace on their own land.

Your Answer _____

_____

Answers

A–43

(B) While modern guns killed many, the use of alcohol destroyed families, and being banished to reservations killed spirits, the author firmly believes that the loss of the buffalo destroyed the societies of the plains nations.

A–44

(B) Option (B) is the only plausible response. In option (A) the facts are confused. It was the killing of 9 million buffalo in three years that contributed greatly to the downward spiral of the Indians' way of life. There had been 13 million roaming in 1850. The Sioux and the Cheyenne fought for their way of life (C). The Victory at Little Big Horn wasn't enough to preserve their freedom. (D)

Q–45

Does the author show any bias in how she has presented her passage?

(A) The author has shown equality in the treatment of all persons cited in her passage.

(B) The author appears to side with the whites who were attempting to make their own life on the plains.

(C) The author's clear bias is toward the Indian inhabitants of the plains whose entire ecosystem was wiped out with the slaughter of the buffalo.

(D) The author believes that the Indians should have accepted their fate so that their tribes and families could live in peace.

Your Answer _____

_____

Answers

A–45

(**C**) The author is very clear in her presentation of facts that she believes that the Indians were wronged, eliminating (A). She doesn't mention the settlers directly (B). And nowhere does she allude to the Indians just giving up. (D)

Questions

Q–46

What is the strongest argument used by the author to support her argument in favor of the Indians?

(A) The Indians were outnumbered and out-gunned.

(B) The white settlers were coming out in large numbers to ranch and farm the land that they believed was theirs.

(C) The decimation of the buffalo herds by the whites destroyed the way of life of the Plains Indians.

(D) It would be better for the Indians to assimilate their culture with that of the whites and live a new way of life without the buffalo.

Your Answer _____

_____

Answers

(C) Answer choices (A) and (B) were definitely a large part of the decline of the way of life of the Plains Indians, but the author specifically claims that the loss of the herds of buffalo was the major cause. Answer choice (D) is what happened to many of the peoples of the plains, but does not accord with what the author would regard as favoring the Indians' interests.

PASSAGE 9

Homeostatic Mechanisms

Laurie A. Callihan, Ph.D.

All human cells, tissues, and organs must maintain a tight range of physical and chemical conditions in order to live and thrive. Conditions such as temperature, pH, water balance, sugar levels, etc., must be monitored and controlled in order to keep them within the accepted ranges that will not inhibit life. When conditions are within acceptable ranges, the body is said to be in homeostasis. The body has a special set of mechanisms that serve to keep it in homeostasis. Homeostasis is a state of dynamic equilibrium, which balances forces tending toward change and forces acceptable for life functions.

Homeostasis is achieved mostly by actions of the sympathetic and parasympathetic nervous systems by a process known as feedback control. For instance, when the body undergoes physical activity, muscle action causes a rise in temperature. Unchecked, rising temperature can destroy cells. In this instance, the nervous system detects rising temperature and reacts with a response that causes sweat glands to produce sweat. The evaporation of sweat cools the body.

There are many instances of feedback control. These take effect when any situation arises that may drive levels out of the normal acceptable range. In other words, the homeostatic mechanism is a reaction to a stimulus. This reaction, called a feedback response, is the production of some counterforce that levels the system.

External environmental conditions can cause feedback responses within the body to attempt to maintain homeostasis. For example, if an individual is exposed to extreme cold, the body will react by constricting blood vessels near the surface of the skin, which causes shivering. Shivering is meant to produce heat and to warm the body back up when the internal temperature begins to drop. If the body core temperature continues to drop, a condition known as hypothermia will occur, metabolic systems will begin to slow down, the heart pumps slower and brain functions become sluggish. If a warm-up does not occur, hypothermia will lead to death. However, the metabolic slow-down preserves organs for a time in hopes of a rescue. In fact, inducing hypothermic states is now used in some lengthy surgeries to maintain the health of organs during high-stress situations.

An injury is an assault on the body's homeostatic mechanisms. When any type of injury occurs, homeostatic mechanisms within the body will set about to make the situation right. For example, if bleeding is occurring, feedback mechanisms go to work that release clotting factors to stop bleeding at the injury site. While the immune system moves to fight infection, homeostatic mechanisms will work to regulate body temperature, chemical concentrations needed for cellular metabolism, etc.

Refer to the above passage for questions 47 – 49.

Questions

Q-47

What does the author say all human cells and tissues must have to live and thrive?

(A) Food and water

(B) Feedback control

(C) Body temperature

(D) A tight range of physical and chemical conditions

Your Answer _____

_____

Q-48

What does the author say can happen if a rising temperature is unchecked?

(A) If unchecked, rising temperature can destroy cells.

(B) Cells will unite to bring down the body's temperature.

(C) The body will begin to sweat in order to cool off.

(D) Cells will shut down, and become reactivated under cooler circumstances.

Your Answer _____

_____

Answers

A–47

(D) In the very first paragraph, the author states that a tight range of physical and chemical conditions must be met for human cells and tissue to thrive. Food and water (A) and body temperature (B) contribute to sustaining life but that isn't the author's central point. Feedback control is not relevant here.

A–48

(A) The important words in the question are "if unchecked." When healthy, the nervous system reacts with a response that causes sweat glands to produce sweat (C).

Questions

Q–49

What definition does the author give for the homeostatic mechanism?

(A)   The homeostatic mechanism is a combining of outer stimuli.

(B)   The homeostatic mechanism is a reaction to a stimulus.

(C)   The homeostatic mechanism comes from external environmental conditions.

(D)   The homeostatic mechanism is hypothermia.

Your Answer _____

_____

Q–50

How is homeostasis achieved?

(A)   Homeostasis is achieved by a process known as feedback control.

(B)   Homeostasis is achieved by a process called homeostatic mechanisms.

(C)   Homeostasis is achieved by a process that drops core body temperature.

(D)   Homeostasis is achieved by a process known as hypothermia.

Your Answer _____

_____

Answers

(B) This answer gives the overall definition of homeostatic mechanism (see paragraph 3). Two other answer choices, (A) and (C), are incomplete. Hypothermia is a condition caused by extreme exposure to cold (D).

A–49

(A) The overall process to achieve homeostasis is called feedback control. The control takes effect when any situation arises that may drive levels out of the normal acceptable range. In other words, the homeostatic mechanism is a reaction to a stimulus. This reaction produces a counterforce that levels the system. (The other answer choices do not apply to this operation.)

Take Quiz 4 at the REA Study Center to test your immediate grasp of the topics in this section.
(www.rea.com/studycenter)

Section V
Writing

ABOUT THE WRITING SUBTEST

The first section you will face on the PCAT exam is the Writing subtest. This test is on the PCAT because the pharmacy college you wish to attend wants to have evidence that you can solve problems, and can write about them capably.

The Writing subtest will contain a prompt addressing health, science, social, cultural, or political issues. Your task will be to offer a possible solution to the problem stated in the prompt. This solution will need to be correct, logical, and convincing. In the 30 minutes allotted for this subtest, you will need to compose, write, and edit your solution. During the test you will be able to cut, copy, and paste. You won't have access to spell check or grammar check.

There is no substitute for practice. Responding to sample prompts will go a long way to improve your fluency and ease any anxiety you might have about this task. Pearson, the PCAT test maker, has some worthwhile sample writing test prompts on its website (*pcatweb.info),* which can be found by clicking on the "resources" tab and choosing "PCAT Test Blueprint and Sample Items."

After you've practiced with a few sample writing prompts, set a timer on your phone, watch, or tablet for 30 minutes to be sure you get your timing down. Break the 30-minute time window into chunks that work best for you. For example: 5 minutes to think and brainstorm; 3 minutes to choose a solution from your brainstorming; 3 minutes to construct an outline; 14 minutes to write; and 5 minutes to proofread and clean up your submission.

Hints to Improve Your Score on the Writing Subtest

- Read, really read the prompt. Do not just glance at it.

- Make notes as you go.

- Decide on your solution.

- Think. Don't just leap into your response. Be sure you're making the best case you can. Use the argument you're most comfortable with.

- Your outline will have to be selective—not everything you know, but what you know that you can state clearly and use to stay on point in the time available. Focus on what you do know about the question, not on what you don't.

- Respond using clear, clean, and specific ideas (no extra fluff.)

- Shore up your ideas. Make them count.

- Be logical. Don't jump all over the place.

- Be clear, clean, and specific (but also effective.)

- Keep it simple. (You are not writing a lawyer's brief!)

- Use a variety of constructions. Everything can't be "I think..."

- Avoid passive voice. Everybody who has ever taught writing says this. But using active voice also tends to help you be less wordy.

- Vary the length of your sentences.

- Don't switch points of view. Stay in the third person as that is the strongest, occasionally use first person, avoid second person.

- Be logical and convincing—you want the reader to feel she learned something.

- No extra words. Use time at the end to delete any extra words you have injected.

- You will make errors as you draft your answer. Save time to hunt and fix them before time runs out. A few minutes of careful proofreading can improve your grade.

You don't have to do all of the above on your first try! Incorporate additional hints as you move forward. Many will come to you naturally. The rest you can work your way up to.

The scores of 1–6 (with 6 as the highest) are based on your actual solution, but also on your use of language conventions such as grammar, style, usage and punctuation. Scorers are not looking for perfection but the ability to problem solve. One scorer of your essay will be a well-trained professional. The second scorer may be Pearson's Intelligent Essay Assessor (IEA), which automatically evaluates the effectiveness of your work as well as your use of grammar, style, and mechanics.

PERIODIC TABLE

Atomic Properties of the Elements

NIST
National Institute of Standards and Technology
U.S. Department of Commerce

Physics Laboratory
physics.nist.gov

Standard Reference Data
www.nist.gov/srd

Frequently used fundamental physical constants

For the most accurate values of these and other constants, visit physics.nist.gov/constants

1 second = 9 192 631 770 periods of radiation corresponding to the transition between the two hyperfine levels of the ground state of ^{133}Cs

speed of light in vacuum	c	299 792 458 $m\ s^{-1}$	(exact)
Planck constant	h	6.6261×10^{-34} J s	($\hbar = h/2\pi$)
elementary charge	e	1.6022×10^{-19} C	
electron mass	m_e	9.1094×10^{-31} kg	
	m_ec^2	0.5110 MeV	
proton mass	m_p	1.6726×10^{-27} kg	
fine-structure constant	α	1/137.036	
Rydberg constant	R_∞	10 973 732 m^{-1}	
	$R_\infty c$	$3.289\ 842 \times 10^{15}$ Hz	
	$R_\infty hc$	13.6057 eV	
Boltzmann constant	k	$1.3807 \times 10^{-23}\ J\ K^{-1}$	

- Solids
- Liquids
- Gases
- Artificially Prepared

Period	Group 1 IA	2 IIA	3 IIIB	4 IVB	5 VB	6 VIB	7 VIIB	8 VIII	9 VIII	10 VIII	11 IB	12 IIB	13 IIIA	14 IVA	15 VA	16 VIA	17 VIIA	18 VIIIA
1	1 $^2S_{1/2}$ **H** Hydrogen 1.00794 $1s$ 13.5984																	2 $^1S_0$ **He** Helium 4.002602 $1s^2$ 24.5874
2	3 $^2S_{1/2}$ **Li** Lithium 6.941 $1s^22s$ 5.3917	4 $^1S_0$ **Be** Beryllium 9.012182 $1s^22s^2$ 9.3227											5 $^2P^\circ_{1/2}$ **B** Boron 10.811 $1s^22s^22p$ 8.2980	6 $^3P_0$ **C** Carbon 12.0107 $1s^22s^22p^2$ 11.2603	7 $^4S^\circ_{3/2}$ **N** Nitrogen 14.0067 $1s^22s^22p^3$ 14.5341	8 $^3P_2$ **O** Oxygen 15.9994 $1s^22s^22p^4$ 13.6181	9 $^2P^\circ_{3/2}$ **F** Fluorine 18.9984032 $1s^22s^22p^5$ 17.4228	10 $^1S_0$ **Ne** Neon 20.1797 $1s^22s^22p^6$ 21.5645
3	11 $^2S_{1/2}$ **Na** Sodium 22.98976928 $[Ne]3s$ 5.1391	12 $^1S_0$ **Mg** Magnesium 24.3050 $[Ne]3s^2$ 7.6462											13 $^2P^\circ_{1/2}$ **Al** Aluminum 26.9815386 $[Ne]3s^23p$ 5.9858	14 $^3P_0$ **Si** Silicon 28.0855 $[Ne]3s^23p^2$ 8.1517	15 $^4S^\circ_{3/2}$ **P** Phosphorus 30.973762 $[Ne]3s^23p^3$ 10.4867	16 $^3P_2$ **S** Sulfur 32.065 $[Ne]3s^23p^4$ 10.3600	17 $^2P^\circ_{3/2}$ **Cl** Chlorine 35.453 $[Ne]3s^23p^5$ 12.9676	18 $^1S_0$ **Ar** Argon 39.948 $[Ne]3s^23p^6$ 15.7596
4	19 $^2S_{1/2}$ **K** Potassium 39.0983 $[Ar]4s$ 4.3407	20 $^1S_0$ **Ca** Calcium 40.078 $[Ar]4s^2$ 6.1132	21 $^2D_{3/2}$ **Sc** Scandium 44.955912 $[Ar]3d4s^2$ 6.5615	22 $^3F_2$ **Ti** Titanium 47.867 $[Ar]3d^24s^2$ 6.8281	23 $^4F_{3/2}$ **V** Vanadium 50.9415 $[Ar]3d^34s^2$ 6.7462	24 $^7S_3$ **Cr** Chromium 51.9961 $[Ar]3d^54s$ 6.7665	25 $^6S_{5/2}$ **Mn** Manganese 54.938045 $[Ar]3d^54s^2$ 7.4340	26 $^5D_4$ **Fe** Iron 55.845 $[Ar]3d^64s^2$ 7.9024	27 $^4F_{9/2}$ **Co** Cobalt 58.933195 $[Ar]3d^74s^2$ 7.8810	28 $^3F_4$ **Ni** Nickel 58.6934 $[Ar]3d^84s^2$ 7.6399	29 $^2S_{1/2}$ **Cu** Copper 63.546 $[Ar]3d^{10}4s$ 7.7264	30 $^1S_0$ **Zn** Zinc 65.38 $[Ar]3d^{10}4s^2$ 9.3942	31 $^2P^\circ_{1/2}$ **Ga** Gallium 69.723 $[Ar]3d^{10}4s^24p$ 5.9993	32 $^3P_0$ **Ge** Germanium 72.64 $[Ar]3d^{10}4s^24p^2$ 7.8994	33 $^4S^\circ_{3/2}$ **As** Arsenic 74.92160 $[Ar]3d^{10}4s^24p^3$ 9.7886	34 $^3P_2$ **Se** Selenium 78.96 $[Ar]3d^{10}4s^24p^4$ 9.7524	35 $^2P^\circ_{3/2}$ **Br** Bromine 79.904 $[Ar]3d^{10}4s^24p^5$ 11.8138	36 $^1S_0$ **Kr** Krypton 83.798 $[Ar]3d^{10}4s^24p^6$ 13.9996
5	37 $^2S_{1/2}$ **Rb** Rubidium 85.4678 $[Kr]5s$ 4.1771	38 $^1S_0$ **Sr** Strontium 87.62 $[Kr]5s^2$ 5.6949	39 $^2D_{3/2}$ **Y** Yttrium 88.90585 $[Kr]4d5s^2$ 6.2173	40 $^3F_2$ **Zr** Zirconium 91.224 $[Kr]4d^25s^2$ 6.6339	41 $^6D_{1/2}$ **Nb** Niobium 92.90638 $[Kr]4d^45s$ 6.7589	42 $^7S_3$ **Mo** Molybdenum 95.96 $[Kr]4d^55s$ 7.0924	43 $^6S_{5/2}$ **Tc** Technetium (98) $[Kr]4d^55s^2$ 7.28	44 $^5F_5$ **Ru** Ruthenium 101.07 $[Kr]4d^75s$ 7.3605	45 $^4F_{9/2}$ **Rh** Rhodium 102.90550 $[Kr]4d^85s$ 7.4589	46 $^1S_0$ **Pd** Palladium 106.42 $[Kr]4d^{10}$ 8.3369	47 $^2S_{1/2}$ **Ag** Silver 107.8682 $[Kr]4d^{10}5s$ 7.5762	48 $^1S_0$ **Cd** Cadmium 112.411 $[Kr]4d^{10}5s^2$ 8.9938	49 $^2P^\circ_{1/2}$ **In** Indium 114.818 $[Kr]4d^{10}5s^25p$ 5.7864	50 $^3P_0$ **Sn** Tin 118.710 $[Kr]4d^{10}5s^25p^2$ 7.3439	51 $^4S^\circ_{3/2}$ **Sb** Antimony 121.760 $[Kr]4d^{10}5s^25p^3$ 8.6084	52 $^3P_2$ **Te** Tellurium 127.60 $[Kr]4d^{10}5s^25p^4$ 9.0096	53 $^2P^\circ_{3/2}$ **I** Iodine 126.90447 $[Kr]4d^{10}5s^25p^5$ 10.4513	54 $^1S_0$ **Xe** Xenon 131.293 $[Kr]4d^{10}5s^25p^6$ 12.1298
6	55 $^2S_{1/2}$ **Cs** Cesium 132.9054519 $[Xe]6s$ 3.8939	56 $^1S_0$ **Ba** Barium 137.327 $[Xe]6s^2$ 5.2117		72 $^3F_2$ **Hf** Hafnium 178.49 $[Xe]4f^{14}5d^26s^2$ 6.8251	73 $^4F_{3/2}$ **Ta** Tantalum 180.94788 $[Xe]4f^{14}5d^36s^2$ 7.5496	74 $^5D_0$ **W** Tungsten 183.84 $[Xe]4f^{14}5d^46s^2$ 7.8640	75 $^6S_{5/2}$ **Re** Rhenium 186.207 $[Xe]4f^{14}5d^56s^2$ 7.8335	76 $^5D_4$ **Os** Osmium 190.23 $[Xe]4f^{14}5d^66s^2$ 8.4382	77 $^4F_{9/2}$ **Ir** Iridium 192.217 $[Xe]4f^{14}5d^76s^2$ 8.9670	78 $^3D_3$ **Pt** Platinum 195.084 $[Xe]4f^{14}5d^96s$ 8.9588	79 $^2S_{1/2}$ **Au** Gold 196.966569 $[Xe]4f^{14}5d^{10}6s$ 9.2255	80 $^1S_0$ **Hg** Mercury 200.59 $[Xe]4f^{14}5d^{10}6s^2$ 10.4375	81 $^2P^\circ_{1/2}$ **Tl** Thallium 204.3833 $[Hg]6p$ 6.1082	82 $^3P_0$ **Pb** Lead 207.2 $[Hg]6p^2$ 7.4167	83 $^4S^\circ_{3/2}$ **Bi** Bismuth 208.98040 $[Hg]6p^3$ 7.2855	84 $^3P_2$ **Po** Polonium (209) $[Hg]6p^4$ 8.414	85 $^2P^\circ_{3/2}$ **At** Astatine (210) $[Hg]6p^5$	86 $^1S_0$ **Rn** Radon (222) $[Hg]6p^6$ 10.7485
7	87 $^2S_{1/2}$ **Fr** Francium (223) $[Rn]7s$ 4.0727	88 $^1S_0$ **Ra** Radium (226) $[Rn]7s^2$ 5.2784		104 $^3F_2$? **Rf** Rutherfordium (265) $[Rn]5f^{14}6d^27s^2$? 6.0?	105 **Db** Dubnium (268)	106 **Sg** Seaborgium (271)	107 **Bh** Bohrium (272)	108 **Hs** Hassium (277)	109 **Mt** Meitnerium (276)	110 **Ds** Darmstadtium (281)	111 **Rg** Roentgenium (280)	112 **Cn** Copernicium (285)	113 **Uut** Ununtrium (284)	114 **Uuq** Ununquadium (289)	115 **Uup** Ununpentium (288)	116 **Uuh** Ununhexium (293)	117 **Uus** Ununseptium (294)	118 **Uuo** Ununoctium (294)

Lanthanides	57 $^2D_{3/2}$ **La** Lanthanum 138.90547 $[Xe]5d6s^2$ 5.5769	58 $^1G^\circ_4$ **Ce** Cerium 140.116 $[Xe]4f5d6s^2$ 5.5387	59 $^4I^\circ_{9/2}$ **Pr** Praseodymium 140.90765 $[Xe]4f^36s^2$ 5.473	60 $^5I_4$ **Nd** Neodymium 144.242 $[Xe]4f^46s^2$ 5.5250	61 $^6H^\circ_{5/2}$ **Pm** Promethium (145) $[Xe]4f^56s^2$ 5.582	62 $^7F_0$ **Sm** Samarium 150.36 $[Xe]4f^66s^2$ 5.6437	63 $^8S^\circ_{7/2}$ **Eu** Europium 151.964 $[Xe]4f^76s^2$ 5.6704	64 $^9D^\circ_2$ **Gd** Gadolinium 157.25 $[Xe]4f^75d6s^2$ 6.1498	65 $^6H^\circ_{15/2}$ **Tb** Terbium 158.92535 $[Xe]4f^96s^2$ 5.8638	66 $^5I_8$ **Dy** Dysprosium 162.500 $[Xe]4f^{10}6s^2$ 5.9389	67 $^4I^\circ_{15/2}$ **Ho** Holmium 164.93032 $[Xe]4f^{11}6s^2$ 6.0215	68 $^3H_6$ **Er** Erbium 167.259 $[Xe]4f^{12}6s^2$ 6.1077	69 $^2F^\circ_{7/2}$ **Tm** Thulium 168.93421 $[Xe]4f^{13}6s^2$ 6.1843	70 $^1S_0$ **Yb** Ytterbium 173.054 $[Xe]4f^{14}6s^2$ 6.2542	71 $^2D_{3/2}$ **Lu** Lutetium 174.9668 $[Xe]4f^{14}5d6s^2$ 5.4259
Actinides	89 $^2D_{3/2}$ **Ac** Actinium (227) $[Rn]6d7s^2$ 5.3807	90 $^3F_2$ **Th** Thorium 232.03806 $[Rn]6d^27s^2$ 6.3067	91 $^4K_{11/2}$ **Pa** Protactinium 231.03588 $[Rn]5f^26d7s^2$ 5.89	92 $^5L^\circ_6$ **U** Uranium 238.02891 $[Rn]5f^36d7s^2$ 6.1939	93 $^6L_{11/2}$ **Np** Neptunium (237) $[Rn]5f^46d7s^2$ 6.2657	94 $^7F_0$ **Pu** Plutonium (244) $[Rn]5f^67s^2$ 6.0260	95 $^8S^\circ_{7/2}$ **Am** Americium (243) $[Rn]5f^77s^2$ 5.9738	96 $^9D^\circ_2$ **Cm** Curium (247) $[Rn]5f^76d7s^2$ 5.9914	97 $^6H^\circ_{15/2}$ **Bk** Berkelium (247) $[Rn]5f^97s^2$ 6.1979	98 $^5I_8$ **Cf** Californium (251) $[Rn]5f^{10}7s^2$ 6.2817	99 $^4I^\circ_{15/2}$ **Es** Einsteinium (252) $[Rn]5f^{11}7s^2$ 6.3676	100 $^3H_6$ **Fm** Fermium (257) $[Rn]5f^{12}7s^2$ 6.50	101 $^2F^\circ_{7/2}$ **Md** Mendelevium (258) $[Rn]5f^{13}7s^2$ 6.58	102 $^1S_0$ **No** Nobelium (259) $[Rn]5f^{14}7s^2$ 6.65	103 $^2P^\circ_{1/2}$? **Lr** Lawrencium (262) $[Rn]5f^{14}7s^27p$? 4.9 ?

Key:

Atomic Number	58
Ground-state Level	$^1G^\circ_4$
Symbol	**Ce**
Name	Cerium
Atomic Weight[†]	140.116
Ground-state Configuration	$[Xe]4f5d6s^2$
Ionization Energy (eV)	5.5387

[†]Based upon ^{12}C. () indicates the mass number of the longest-lived isotope.

For a description of the data, visit physics.nist.gov/data

NIST SP 966 (September 2010)